Money for Life Success Planner

A 12-Week Companion to Achieve Financial Fitness

Steven B. Smith

Dearborn™
Trade Publishing
A Kaplan Professional Company

Vice President and Publisher: Cynthia A. Zigmund
Acquisitions Editor: Mary B. Good
Senior Managing Editor: Jack Kiburz
Interior Design: Lucy Jenkins
Cover Design: DePinto Studios
Typesetting: the dotted i
Graphic design: Jennifer Streiff

Published by Dearborn Trade Publishing
A Kaplan Professional Company

Printed in the United States of America

05 06 10 9 8 7 6 5 4 3 2

Library of Congress Cataloging-in-Publication Data

Smith, Steven B., 1966–
Money for life success planner : a 12-week companion to achieve financial fitness / Steven B. Smith.
p. cm.
A companion to the author's Money for life.
ISBN 0-7931-9515-2 (pbk.)
1. Finance, Personal. 2. Financial security. I. Smith, Steven B., 1966– . Money for life. II. Title.
HG179.S55135 2004
332.024'01—dc22

2004014932

Dearborn Trade books are available at special quantity discounts to use for sales promotions, employee premiums, or educational purposes. Please call our Special Sales Department to order or for more information at 800-621-9621, ext. 4444, e-mail trade@dearborn.com, or write to Dearborn Trade Publishing, 30 South Wacker Drive, Suite 2500, Chicago, IL 60606-7481.

This book is dedicated to those who have
a dream to pursue,
the vision to plan,
the courage to run,
the expectation to perfect,
and the persistence to win!

Contents

List of Figures

Prologue

Laying the Foundation for Success

Plan and Track

Week 5

Appendix A: Mvelopes® Personal—An Envelope System for Today's World

Appendix B: Forms

Acknowledgments

I am grateful for the assistance and support of many people without whom this project would not have become a reality.

Particularly, I am grateful to:

- Richard Kuhn and David Neddo for their collective vision and assistance in creating the outline and material used to complete the *Money for Life Success Planner.*
- Jennifer Streiff and Debby Josephson for their assistance in creating successful form and function from raw ideas and concepts. This project is a success because of their energy and dedication.
- The In2M management team for their collective vision, passion, hard work, and outstanding support from day one.
- The In2M employees who work tirelessly every day to make visions and dreams become a reality for our customers.
- My business partners and In2M shareholders—without their continued support, this project would not have been possible.
- My editor, Mary Good, and the rest of a very qualified and professional organization at Dearborn. Their insight, energy, passion, and dedication to this project have been extraordinary. I thank them for making this project both a success and a great pleasure.
- Finally, to my wife, Jana. The success of this project is yet another example of what can be accomplished when you have the love and support of a patient companion.

Preface

Achieving any type of success usually requires the application of sound principles, proper planning, careful tracking, and appropriate adjustments along the way. In the book *Money for Life: Budgeting Success and Financial Fitness in Just 12 Weeks,* Ryan and Christine Richardson learned valuable lessons about the principles, tools, and steps necessary to successfully achieve personal financial fitness.

Ryan and Christine once enjoyed a solid relationship. They were educated, had a good income, and were focused on successfully raising a family. Like so many in similar situations, they had allowed financial stress and frustration to erode their happiness. Finally, understanding the perilous direction in which they were headed—spending more money than they made—Ryan and Christine Richardson decided to change their financial course. With the help of a wise financial advisor, they learned how to achieve financial fitness through the implementation of a back-to-basics budgeting approach based on the timeless "envelope" method of budgeting. Their story is a fictional one, but they, like thousands of their real-life counterparts, found that there really is a way to live within your income, enabling the creation of stability and long-term financial fitness.

The secret is spending less than you make. Although this may sound like a simple thing to do, it is surprisingly complex in this ever-changing and expanding "cashless" electronic society. However, doing this consistently for several years will help to create a level of financial security most people only dream about. It requires the consistent application of the principles and steps that you will learn here in the *Money for Life Success Planner.* Everyone needs to develop a spending plan regardless of how much they make. Whether you use cash, paper and pencil, a spreadsheet, software, or something else, you need to do something. And you need to get started now—it's that important.

The *Success Planner* has been developed to assist you with the objective of achieving financial fitness. Carefully completing the activities and exercises contained in this planner helps you follow the same path to financial fitness that Ryan and Christine followed. You will be amazed, as they were, how many significant and positive changes can be made in just a few short weeks.

This *Success Planner* guides you through the 12-week financial fitness program outlined in *Money for Life*. When you have finished the program, this planner allows you to retrace your steps, as well as review the adjustments and changes you have made. You will be able to understand and see clearly, not only how your thought processes and behaviors have changed, but also how your new thought processes and behaviors have led you to a level of financial fitness that you perhaps did not think was possible. Specifically, you will be able to:

- Spend less than you make.
- Plan for unexpected expenses, including emergencies.
- Set money aside in advance of spending requirements.
- Implement a household budgeting system that makes communicating easy, even fun.
- Put a plan in place for debt elimination.
- Use credit cards without increasing debt.
- Successfully manage your money in today's "cashless" electronic society.

This exciting journey is yours and yours alone. No one else can make it for you. The satisfaction and peace that you achieve will be a direct result of the energy and dedication you apply. I am excited about your journey down the financial path least traveled. Thousands have gone before you, and thousands are joining you every day. The rewards will truly be extraordinary. Congratulations on choosing to become financially fit!

Introduction

The *Money for Life Success Planner* has been designed to assist you with implementing a 12-week financial fitness program, the same program that Ryan and Christine Richardson followed in the book *Money for Life.* As you continue through the *Success Planner,* you will see references to *Money for Life.* Each time you see this symbol $, you will be referred to specific sections within the book for further reading and information. This information is meant to supplement your experience with the *Success Planner* and allows you to refer to specific applied principles and educational topics for further review and study.

Each section of the *Success Planner* outlines exercises and activities that are important for you to follow at each stage. The first section helps you lay the foundation for your success by assisting you to prepare for the following 12 weeks. You assess your current level of financial fitness by completing a personal financial fitness questionnaire together with an initial net-worth statement. You then prepare a list of personal financial objectives to help guide your thinking and focus your efforts.

The sections corresponding to weeks 1 through 12 represent your 12-week effort. Each section outlines the activities and exercises to be followed for that week. You also receive guidance for using your chosen envelope system. There are many methods by which you can successfully implement the envelope budgeting principles including cash, paper ledger, computer spreadsheet, or a computer-based system like Mvelopes® Personal. The *Success Planner* focuses on two implementation methods: paper ledger and Mvelopes Personal. All of the forms necessary to adopt the paper ledger method have been provided, including those forms needed to assist you with the development of a spending plan as well as an allocation plan, which is also commonly known as a funding plan. Please feel free to copy the forms as necessary to ensure you have enough of each one. The CD included with the book *Money for Life* allows you to use Mvelopes Personal. If you did not receive a CD, visit http://www.mvelopes.com/moneyforlife for information on how to begin using the Mvelopes Personal spending management system. If you choose to use Mvelopes Personal as your implementation method, watch for the screened

$ **Money *for* Life**
Appendix B, pages 155–65

boxes throughout the *Success Planner*. Each time this symbol Mvelopes Personal appears, you will see a reference to a specific section of the Mvelopes Personal Tutorial. The tutorial is a multimedia demonstration of how to use Mvelopes Personal and can be accessed within the Mvelopes Personal system

As you move through the 12-week program, you will read about real-life success stories. You will likely relate to many of these individuals and families, as their financial circumstances are similar to countless others, and many of the obstacles and challenges that they face are probably similar to yours.

The final two sections of the *Success Planner* contain information and exercises designed to assist you in reviewing your success, and in planning for your ongoing approach to maintaining and increasing financial fitness beyond the initial 12 weeks. You will learn the importance of continuing on the path that you have chosen to ensure long-term success. Following this program allows you to transform your personal financial life and create a level of peace and happiness that few others enjoy. With *Money for Life* as an educational resource, and the *Success Planner* as your implementation guide, you are well on your way to becoming financially fit and to securing long-term financial freedom. There is no time like the present, so let's get started!

Prologue

Money *for* Life

Applied Principles 6 and 7, pages 44–51

One of the most common misconceptions in our society is that having higher levels of income automatically translates into the creation of greater levels of wealth. Thomas J. Stanley and William D. Danko found this not to be the case for the vast majority of individuals and families. The comprehensive study they conducted and outlined in their bestselling book, *The Millionaire Next Door,* clearly demonstrated that wealth is not so much a function of how much money we make but rather how we choose to spend the money that we do make. Stanley and Danko found that the path to substantial net worth was similar for many wealthy people in America. Most had modest incomes and had accumulated their wealth over a number of years. These individuals and families had mastered the ability to live within their means. Ultimately, they were able to spend less than they made on a consistent basis. People will be much more successful in achieving true long-term financial fitness if they focus first on living within their means. The secret lies in the way all of us choose to spend our money rather than in the way we choose to earn our money.

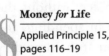

In the book *Money for Life,* Ryan and Christine Richardson found that when they applied the principle of spending less than they made, they could quickly become more financially fit. Within a short period, the Richardsons were able to begin rapidly reducing their consumer debt. With the application of the debt roll-down principle discussed in the book *Money for Life,* they were on track to completely eliminate all debt, including their mortgage, in less than nine years.

Money *for* Life

Applied Principle 15, pages 116–19

Consistently living within your means and rapidly reducing your debt load are the keys to increasing your net worth in a meaningful way. This prudent approach to your personal finances has the potential of changing your life for the better, now and in the future.

Before making a commitment to change their approach, Ryan and Christine were on the financial path most traveled. Ultimately this path was creating significant levels of discontent in their relationship. It was also contributing to high and increasing levels of debt. They struggled with making payments on time, had little to no savings, and had no resources set aside to handle financial emergencies. It was a struggle every day to make financial ends meet. They thought that an increase in income would solve their problems, but even when Christine returned to work after taking time off to have their two children, they were unable to keep their spending in check.

The Richardsons' approach to personal finances was very similar to most people's approach in our society. We constantly tell ourselves we will eliminate our debt when we earn more money, falsely believing that we will be able to save more money in the future. We lull ourselves into a false sense of security, believing we will be able to put more money away for retirement as our income increases. However, every day many people in our society are finding that the future comes very quickly, and often without warning. They are startled by the grim reality that they are facing retirement, or other significant financial requirements, without adequate resources while still maintaining high levels of debt.

The Richardsons were able to change financial directions and begin laying the foundation for long-term financial fitness and ultimately financial security when they made the commitment to live within their means and rapidly eliminate debt. When the Richardsons began their journey down the path to true financial fitness and long-term financial security, they had a net worth of approximately $20,000. They made a commitment to live within their means and eliminate their debt within 9 years. They also made a commitment to develop a plan to retire comfortably within 30 years, or by the time Ryan turned 65. Their current household annual net income was approximately $75,000, which included both Ryan's and Christine's salaries. If the Richardsons are able to continue on their current path for the next 30 years, they will be in a remarkably comfortable position at the time they retire. Figure P.1 outlines the Richardsons' net-worth statement at different points in time for the next 30 years.

This example assumes that the Richardsons are able to achieve the objective of completely eliminating their debt within 9 years. It also assumes their net income grows by 3.5 percent each year for the next 20 years and then remains static for the remaining 10 years. The example also assumes that the Richardsons' spending levels increase annually by 3.5 percent for the first 20 years and then by 1.5 percent for the remaining 10 years. It further assumes a modest 6 percent return on the Richardsons' investment accounts. As you can see, without the burden of debt and with modest, but appropriate, increases in spending, the Richardsons are able to achieve a net worth of about $3 million at the time they retire. If they continue earning 6 percent on their investments after they retire, they will generate approximately $124,000 in annual net income, not including distributions from Social Security. Given their annual spending levels at retirement of $84,000, the Richardsons will be able to continue their existing standard of living indefinitely and at the same time experience ongoing growth in their asset base. If over the 30-year period prior to retirement the Richardsons achieve an average annual return of 10 percent on their investments, at retirement they would have a net worth of approximately $4.8 million. If this rate of return continued into retirement, they would be able to generate approximately $226,000 in annual net income from their investment accounts.

FIGURE P.1 Richardsons' Progressive Net-Worth Statement

Progressive Personal Income and Net-Worth Statement (Ryan and Christine Richardson)						
Annual Income & Spending	Current	Year 1	Year 5	Year 10	Year 20	Year 30
Annual Net Income	$74,835	$77,501	$88,934	$102,692	$140,718	$140,718
Annual Outflow						
Annual Spending	$45,215	$36,522	$43,826	$50,939	$71,855	$83,390
Annual Debt Service	37,104	37,104	37,104			
Annual Savings/Investments		3,875	8,004	51,753	68,863	57,328
Total Annual Outflow	$82,319	$77,501	$88,934	$102,692	$140,718	$140,718
Total Annual Deficit	($7,484)					
Net-Worth Calculations	Current	Year 1	Year 5	Year 10	Year 20	Year 30
Assets						
Cash-Equivalent Assets						
Checking Account		$2,000	$10,000	$10,000	$10,000	$10,000
Savings Account	$2,300	4,198	22,082	23,208	25,636	28,318
Investment Accounts	5,000	5,300	6,691	111,060	991,879	2,609,525
Total Cash-Equiv. Assets	$7,300	$11,498	$38,773	$144,268	$1,027,514	$2,647,843
Real Estate Assets						
Primary Residence	$225,000	$228,375	$242,389	$261,122	$303,042	$351,693
Other Real Estate Inv.						
Total Real Estate Assets	$225,000	$228,375	$242,389	$261,122	$303,042	$351,693
Other Assets						
Total Other Assets	$32,400	$29,160	$19,132	$25,603	$45,851	$82,112
Total Assets	$264,700	$269,033	$300,294	$430,993	$1,376,407	$3,081,648
Total Liabilities	$244,535	$217,364	$108,680			
TOTAL NET WORTH	$20,165	$51,669	$191,614	$430,993	$1,376,407	$3,081,648

By way of contrast, let's now look at an example of a couple that earns significantly more money than the Richardsons do. Scott and Mary Jacobsen believe that they are living the American dream. As their income has grown, so have both their spending and debt levels. For the past several years, they have consistently spent more than they have earned. Even though their current annual net income is $153,000, they have a net worth of only $59,000, due in large part to their $427,000 debt load. Figure P.2 outlines the net-worth statement for Scott and Mary Jacobsen at various points over the next 30 years.

Like the Richardsons, the Jacobsens experience an annual increase in net income of 3.5 percent each year for the next 20 years. Their net income then remains static at approximately $290,000 for the remaining 10 years. However, unlike the Richardsons, Scott and Mary continue to spend about 5 percent more than they make for several years, making it very difficult for them to save and invest meaningfully. In addition to this spending, the Jacobsens purchase a much larger new home in 10 years with a 30-year mortgage. Scott and Mary also drive nice cars, which they upgrade every 5 years and finance on 5-year loans. Assuming the Jacobsens also achieve an average annual return of 6 percent on their investments, according to our example, they will have a net worth of approximately

FIGURE P.2 Jacobsens' Progressive Net-Worth Statement

Progressive Personal Income and Net-Worth Statement (Scott and Mary Jacobsen)						
Annual Income & Spending	Current	Year 1	Year 5	Year 10	Year 20	Year 30
Annual Net Income	$153,000	$158,355	$181,716	$212,648	$291,007	$291,007
Annual Outflow						
Annual Spending	$101,256	$106,625	$112,602	$142,133	$168,335	$168,335
Annual Debt Service	51,774	51,730	61,845	57,756	81,213	81,248
Annual Savings/Investments	7,650	7,918	16,354	23,391	41,459	41,423
Total Annual Outflow	$160,650	$166,273	$190,802	$223,280	$291,007	$291,007
Total Annual Deficit	($7,650)	($7,918)	($9,086)	($10,632)		
Net-Worth Calculations	Current	Year 1	Year 5	Year 10	Year 20	Year 30
Assets						
Cash-Equivalent Assets						
Checking Account		$2,000	$12,000	$14,000	$14,000	$14,000
Savings Account	$5,000	10,968	54,078	56,836	62,793	69,351
Investment Accounts	10,000	10,600	13,382	139,404	622,110	1,672,182
Total Cash-Equiv. Assets	$15,000	$23,568	$79,460	$210,240	$698,893	$1,755,533
Real Estate Assets						
Primary Residence	$406,250	$412,344	$437,647	$650,000	$754,352	$875,456
Other Real Estate Inv.						
Total Real Estate Assets	$406,250	$412,344	$437,647	$650,000	$754,352	$875,456
Other Assets						
Total Other Assets	$65,000	$58,500	$116,725	$133,346	$179,205	$240,837
Total Assets	$486,250	$494,412	$633,832	$993,586	$1,632,450	$2,871,826
Total Liabilities	$427,150	$415,980	$414,326	$663,368	$627,138	$448,113
TOTAL NET WORTH	$59,100	$78,431	$219,506	$330,218	$1,005,312	$2,423,713

$2.4 million at the time they retire in 30 years, a large portion of which is their $875,000 home. However, when Scott and Mary retire, they will still have a debt load of approximately $450,000. At retirement they will be spending nearly $250,000 annually to fund their lifestyle, including approximately $81,000 in annual debt service. If at retirement they continue making 6 percent annually on their investment accounts, they will have an annual net income of approximately $80,000, not including distributions from Social Security. If the Jacobsens continue living the lifestyle they have grown accustomed to, including the continued service of their debt load, their cash-equivalent assets will be depleted in just over 6 years postretirement.

At the same time, the Richardsons' cash-equivalent assets will have grown by nearly $400,000 to a total value of just under $3 million. See Figure P.3 for a postretirement comparison of the value of the cash-equivalent assets of the Richardsons with those of the Jacobsens.

The contrast between the Richardsons' retirement situation and that of Scott and Mary Jacobsen is sobering. The key to achieving the extraordinary results experienced by the Richardsons in our example is, first, make a commitment to consistently spend less than you make; second, rapidly eliminate the burden of

FIGURE P.3 Financial Comparison of the Richardsons and Jacobsens at Retirement

Financial Comparison at Retirement		
	Ryan and Christine Richardson	Scott and Mary Jacobsen
Value of Cash-Equivalent Assets at Age 65	$2,647,843	$1,755,533
Value of Cash-Equivalent Assets at Age 71	$2,974,780	$167,476

debt; and third, as debt is eliminated, increase the amount you are contributing to prudent savings and investments. The key to achieving each of these once you have made a commitment to do so is utilizing the tools that make success possible. This means adopting the envelope method of planning and spending management. After completing the 12-week program outlined in the *Success Planner,* you will be well on your way to securing true financial fitness and long-term financial security.

Laying the Foundation for Success ■

Sometimes the most difficult part of any worthwhile journey is just getting started. Often the tasks ahead seem daunting—even impossible. If you break down the tasks into manageable pieces, however, you can more easily achieve success. The *Success Planner* has been developed to assist you in following this process.

In this section, you will work through activities that will help you understand your current personal financial position and lay the foundation for successfully achieving financial fitness going forward.

■ ACTION 1—LAYING THE FOUNDATION FOR SUCCESS: Make a Commitment to Change Your Financial Direction

Money *for* Life

Applied Principles 4 and 5, pages 24–27, and "The Principles of Money for Life," page 134

The personal financial path least traveled is the personal financial path we should seek. This takes courage, commitment, and often a change in thinking. Albert Einstein once said: "The significant problems we face cannot be solved at the same level of thinking we were at when we created them." Becoming financially fit often requires us to break from our old thought processes in order to forge new habits and behaviors. You must have the courage and commitment to make these changes. You must be prepared to win the battle of the mind before you can move on to the battle of the checkbook.

Place a check next to each of the following statements showing your commitment to change your financial direction and become financially fit:

___ I/We will evaluate my/our old thought processes and be prepared to make necessary adjustments in my/our thinking where appropriate.

___ I/We will evaluate my/our existing financial habits and behaviors and be prepared to forge new habits and behaviors where appropriate.

■ ACTION 2—LAYING THE FOUNDATION FOR SUCCESS: Take the Financial Fitness Quiz

Have you ever heard the statement *I can't see the forest for the trees?* This statement has much to do with the reason many of us struggle with making appropriate adjustments in our thought processes, and consequently our habits and behaviors. We get so caught up in our existing life, the stresses and frustrations of our current situation, the reality of complex and difficult financial management issues, and everything else in life that makes focusing on personal financial fitness difficult—our trees—that we fail to stand back and see the picture for what it really is. If we take the time to candidly assess our situation, we will be better prepared to make necessary adjustments. This was certainly the case for Ryan and Christine and doubtless would have continued to be the case had Tom, a wise financial advisor, not assisted them in fully understanding their personal financial situation within the complete context of where they should be.

To assist you with your own candid assessment, take the financial fitness quiz. Answer the questions honestly and determine your score accurately. If your finances are combined with someone else's, it might be interesting to have your partner take the quiz independently and then compare your answers and scores. Use one of the Financial Fitness Quiz Scorecards found in Appendix B to record your answers and calculate your score.

Financial Fitness Quiz

1. What percentage of your income have you saved during the last six months?
   a. 10 percent or more b. Less than 10 percent c. None

2. How many times during the last six months has one of your credit cards or store cards reached its maximum limit?
   a. None b. One to two c. Three or more

3. How many times during the last six months has one of your bank accounts been overdrawn?
   a. None b. One to two c. Three or more

4. How many times during the last six months has a bill been paid late?
   a. None b. One to five c. Six or more

5. How many credit cards and/or store cards do you have for personal use?
   a. Three or fewer b. Four to six c. Seven or more

6. If you lost your source of income, how many months could you provide for all of your basic needs and meet each of your financial obligations?
   a. Three or more b. One to three c. Less than one

7. When a credit card or store card is used to make a purchase, how often is the entire balance paid the following month?
   a. Always b. Sometimes c. Never

8. If a major appliance purchase or repair, auto repair, or home repair were suddenly required, what source of money would be used to pay for it?
   a. Funds already on hand
   b. Funds from available credit
   c. No funds available without establishing additional credit

9. If you are single, how frequently during the last six months have you spent time reviewing your financial situation and making financial decisions? If you have a partner, how frequently during the last six months have you spent time with your partner reviewing your joint financial situation and making joint financial decisions?
   a. Weekly b. Monthly c. Rarely to not at all

10. How many times during the last year have you spent time with your partner reviewing your retirement plan? If you are single, how many times have you spent time reviewing your own retirement plan?
    a. One or more
    b. None
    c. Don't have a retirement plan

11. Have you created a written budget during the last 12 months?
    a. Yes
    b. I have a budget, but its not written out.
    c. What budget? I once rented a car from Budget; does that count?

12. How often is a monthly budget used to manage household spending?
    a. Almost always
    b. Sometimes
    c. Rarely to never

13. What information do you most often use to determine if regular household purchases can be made?
    a. The balance remaining in the budget
    b. The balance remaining in a bank account, credit card, or store card
    c. Little to no information—spending is so much easier when I don't think about it!

14. The insurance I have to cover the loss of major assets, including real estate, autos, and personal property, is:
    a. Enough to cover the replacement cost
    b. Less than enough to cover the replacement cost
    c. An amount that I'm unsure about, or I don't have coverage

15. The insurance I have to cover the loss of life is:
    a. Enough to cover internment costs and adequately replace my income for remaining dependents
    b. Enough to cover internment costs but not enough to adequately replace my income for remaining dependents
    c. An amount that I am unsure about, or I don't have coverage

16. The insurance I have to cover a disability is:
    a. Enough to adequately replace my current income
    b. Less than enough to adequately replace my current income
    c. An amount that I'm unsure of, or I don't have coverage

17. The last time a major purchase was made, the primary consideration was:
    a. The total purchase price relative to available funds
    b. The monthly payment relative to available monthly cash flow
    c. The monthly payment without a complete understanding of its impact

18. Most major purchases are:
    a. Planned and saved for
    b. Planned but not adequately saved for
    c. Unplanned and spontaneous—hey, they're giving out free hotdogs at the local furniture store; let's go check out the deals on big-screen TVs

19. How often do you check to make sure you have adequate funds in your bank account(s)?
    a. They usually don't need to be checked because I always have adequate funds.
    b. Weekly
    c. Almost daily

20. How often are issues related to finances the root of conflict in your household?
    a. Rarely if ever
    b. A few times each month
    c. Frequently—we just installed a boxing ring in the family room right in front of the new big-screen TV!

21. How is your overall financial situation this year compared with last year at this time?
    a. Better   b. About the same   c. Worse

22. When I think about my ability to meet future financial obligations for major items (like education or major purchases, etc.), I am:
    a. Completely at ease
    b. Moderately concerned
    c. Very much concerned

23. When I think about my ability to meet future financial obligations and maintain an acceptable lifestyle at retirement, I am:
    a. Completely at ease
    b. Moderately concerned
    c. Very much concerned

24. My approach to personal financial management is:
    a. Proactive—most things are managed according to a plan
    b. Reactive—the squeaky wheel gets the grease
    c. Avoidance—if I don't think about it, perhaps it will go away

25. When I think about my level of personal financial fitness, I feel:
    a. Financially fit—I could keep running forever!
    b. Moderate to weak—I really should get to the gym more often and use that membership I purchased a year ago, because I'm going to faint if I have to run much longer.
    c. Desperate—where's the ambulance? I need to go to the emergency room *now*!

Scoring: Count the number of a, b, and c answers and follow the formula below to calculate your score.

a. _______ × 1 = _______
b. _______ × 3 = _______
c. _______ × 5 = _______

Total = _______

Check your score according to the following key:

Score	*Level of Financial Fitness*
30 or less	Very high
31 to 50	High
51 to 70	Moderate
71 to 100	Low
101 to 125	Very low

Understanding Your Score

Very high. If your financial fitness score is "Very high," use the *Success Planner* to solidify your current financial habits and behaviors. Look for ways to adopt methods of financial management that will ensure your continued financial fitness long into the future.

Moderate to high. If your financial fitness score is "Moderate" or "High," use the *Success Planner* to look for new ways to increase your financial fitness. Much of what you are doing is placing you on the right path; with some additional adjustments, however, you can move to a higher level of financial fitness. The *Success Planner* will help you along the way.

Low to very low. If your financial fitness score is "Low" or "Very low," use the *Success Planner* to learn and adopt the principles and methods that will assist you with developing new thought processes, behaviors, and habits. You need to place yourself on a new financial path, and the *Success Planner* and your 12-week financial fitness program will help you be successful with this objective.

■ ACTION 3—LAYING THE FOUNDATION FOR SUCCESS: Create a List of Financial Objectives

Money *for* Life

Applied Principle 4, pages 24–26

Perhaps the financial fitness quiz helped focus your thoughts on the areas in your financial life that you would most like to change. Understanding what these areas are and then making a commitment to change them are very important steps in achieving success. Many financial objectives are worthy of personal commitment. The goals and objectives you define at this stage will help further focus your efforts as you continue on your new path. Write down the things you would most like to change in your financial life. These could include:

- No longer living paycheck to paycheck
- Having the money saved for your next vacation before you leave
- Having the money saved for holiday expenses before the spending is required
- Paying cash for your next vehicle purchase
- Reducing or eliminating consumer debt
- Saving for long-term spending requirements, including college and retirement
- Being able to travel without going into debt
- Having money set aside for emergencies
- Creating and living within a budget
- Purchasing only those things you can truly afford
- Working together with your partner to achieve financial goals
- Eliminating the fear, uncertainty, and doubt surrounding finances

- Having the peace and happiness that comes from knowing you are financially fit
- No longer spending more than you make

Write down a list of financial objectives—things in your financial life that you would most like to change or achieve:

1. ______________________________

   ____

2. ______________________________

   ____

3. ______________________________

   ____

4. ______________________________

   ____

5. ______________________________

   ____

6. ______________________________

   ____

7. ______________________________

   ____

■ ACTION 4—LAYING THE FOUNDATION FOR SUCCESS: Create a List of Potential Obstacles

Have you ever noticed that when you make new commitments, it seems that obstacles immediately start getting in the way of success? Many things will try your commitment, including the thoughts, behaviors, and habits that accompanied you on your previous financial path.

With any new goal or commitment, it is very important to anticipate the obstacles you may face and prepare to avoid or altogether eliminate them. This will help ensure your success as you become entangled in the everyday things that often stand in our way. Anticipating these obstacles is not easy, but if you take a good look at past experience, you can successfully identify most of the pitfalls. These may include unexpected events, the temptation to keep up with the purchasing habits of neighbors and coworkers, or invitations to participate in unplanned social outings or travel. By listing these obstacles, you can prepare mentally to address them as they arise.

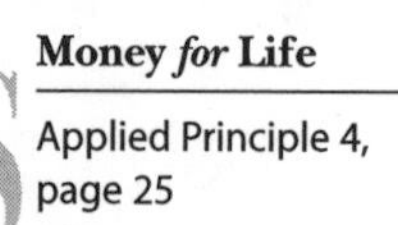
Money *for* Life

Applied Principle 4, page 25

Together with your partner, if applicable, write down a list of the potential obstacles that may stand in the way of successfully achieving the personal financial objectives you have identified. Include the things that have knocked you off course in the past:

1. ____

____

2. ____

____

3. ____

____

4. ____

____

5. ____

____

6. ____

____

■ ACTION 5—LAYING THE FOUNDATION FOR SUCCESS: Make a Commitment to Complete the 12-Week *Money for Life* Program

Any decision to change direction or refocus efforts requires courage and fortitude. Generally, resistance to change is the strongest within the first several weeks of moving down a new path. However, for any worthwhile change in direction to take root, an initial commitment of several weeks must be made. This initial thrust must be long enough to overcome the natural resistance you may have to change. Creating new thought processes, behaviors, and habits does take time, but in as few as 12 short weeks, a significant change in your personal financial health can take place. As you move down the path during this initial 12-week period, you will find that it becomes easier and easier to achieve your objectives. Once your thoughts, actions, and habits become aligned with your financial fitness objectives, you will be able to achieve extraordinary things. Such success comes only to those who are willing to sail through a few short weeks of stormy weather on their path to a safe financial harbor.

Money *for* Life

Applied Principle 17, page 132

With your partner, if applicable, make a commitment to follow and complete the 12-Week *Money for Life* Financial Fitness Program and do what is necessary to achieve your stated financial objectives:

> I/We will do what is necessary to achieve my/our stated financial objectives, including following the 12-Week *Money for Life* Financial Fitness Program. My/Our 12-Week *Money for Life* Program will begin on Sunday, ____________ (month) ___ (day) and will end on Saturday, ___________ (month) ___ (day).

________________________ Signature   ____________ Date

________________________ Spouse/Partner   ____________ Date

It is best to begin after you have taken at least one week to complete Actions 1–10 in the "Laying the Foundation for Success" section. Also, because many people plan and manage their personal finances on a monthly basis, it may be best to begin your 12-week program at the start of the first week of a new month. If it is currently midmonth, you can use the remaining time to complete this section and further review your current financial situation. You can begin to collect information surrounding your current spending levels and debt obligations. This information will be used in the next section.

ACTION 6—LAYING THE FOUNDATION FOR SUCCESS: Prepare a Net-Worth Statement

Before you can move forward in a meaningful way, you need to candidly assess your current financial position. Your initial personal net-worth statement is much the same as an initial physical fitness assessment generated before starting a new physical fitness program. Many financial professionals view your net-worth statement as the measurement of your personal wealth. A positive net worth indicates that the monetary value of your assets is greater than the total of all your liabilities. Negative net worth indicates you owe more in debt than the total monetary value of what you own.

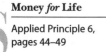

Money *for* Life
Applied Principle 6, pages 44–49

Complete your initial net-worth statement using one of the blank net-worth statement forms found in Appendix B of the *Success Planner.* Completing a net-worth statement isn't difficult and can be done in a short amount of time by following three simple steps.

STEP 1: Create a List of Your Assets and Their Corresponding Values

The first list to compile is your cash-equivalent assets. These assets include the balance in your checking accounts, savings accounts, 401(k) accounts, and IRA accounts; the cash value of life insurance policies; and the current market value of stocks, bonds, or other marketable securities. You may also include in this list money owed to you as long as you have a reasonable likelihood of collecting the outstanding balance. (See Figure LF.1 for an example of cash-equivalent assets.)

The second list to compile is a list of your real estate holdings, which includes the market value of your home and any other property you own. To approximate the value of the real estate you own, you can check with the Realtor who sold you the house or a Realtor who works in your neighborhood. A Realtor can quickly complete a competitive market analysis for you. And in most cases they are quite willing to help. You may also have a recent appraisal report on hand, which would give you an approximate value as well. You need to exercise caution if your recent appraisal was completed as part of a home equity loan or a refinance of

FIGURE LF.1 Cash-Equivalent Assets

Personal Net-Worth Statement	
Assets	Value of Asset
Cash-Equivalent	
Savings Account	$2,300.00
401(k) Accounts	5,000.00
Total Cash-Equivalent	$7,300.00

your existing mortgage as these appraisals can often be 2 to 10 percent high. (See Figure LF.2 for an example of real estate assets.)

The final list of assets would be an itemization of personal property, which would include the current value of vehicles, furniture, and such higher-priced personal property as recreation vehicles, jewelry, collectibles, and perhaps electronic equipment. To determine the current value of your vehicles, visit http://www.bluebook.com and provide the required information. To approximate the value of other personal property, subtract 25 percent of the purchase price for each year you have owned the item. Jewelry and collectibles generally retain their value much better than do furniture and other personal property. Using the purchase price of these items is a safe approximation of their value. If they were received as a gift, you may need to hire a professional to assess their value. (See Figure LF.3.)

FIGURE LF.2 Real Estate Assets

Personal Net-Worth Statement	
Real Estate	Value of Asset
Primary Residence	$225,000.00
Total Real Estate	$225,000.00

FIGURE LF.3 Other Assets

Personal Net-Worth Statement	
Other	Value of Asset
Autos	$17,400.00
Misc. Personal Property	15,000.00
Total Other	$32,400.00

STEP 2: Complete a List of All Debt Obligations (Liabilities)

Create a list of all of your debt obligations. Start with the current amount you owe on your house, home equity loans, and debt consolidation loans. Then list the amount you owe on vehicle loans. Finally, list the balance owed to all consumer debt accounts, including personal loans, student loans, charge accounts, credit card accounts, and any other type of consumer debt. You should be able to find the current balance for each of your debts by checking your most recent statement or by checking for the balance online. (See Figure LF.4.)

FIGURE LF.4 Liabilities (Debt Obligations)

Personal Net-Worth Statement	
Liabilities	Amount of Liability
Mortgage	$206,320.00
Home Equity Loan	9,875.00
American Express	4,855.00
Auto Loan	14,750.00
Visa	4,350.00
Student Loan	3,950.00
Department Store	435.00
Total Liabilities	$244,535.00

STEP 3: Calculate Your Net Worth

To finalize the calculation of your net worth, total the value of all assets listed. Then total the amount of all liabilities listed. Once you have completed these calculations, subtract the total amount of your liabilities from the total value of your assets. The resulting number is an approximation of your current net worth. (See Figure LF.5.)

FIGURE LF.5 Net-Worth Calculation

Personal Net-Worth Statement		
Assets	Value of Asset	
Cash-Equivalent		
Savings Account	$2,300.00	
401(k) Accounts	5,000.00	
Total Cash-Equivalent	$7,300.00	
Real Estate		
Primary Residence	$225,000.00	
Total Real Estate	$225,000.00	
Other		
Autos	$17,400.00	
Misc. Personal Property	15,000.00	
Total Other	$32,400.00	
Total Assets (Cash-Equivalent + Real Estate + Other)		$264,700.00
Liabilities	Amount of Liability	
Mortgage	$206,320.00	
Home Equity Loan	9,875.00	
American Express	4,855.00	
Auto Loan	14,750.00	
Visa	4,350.00	
Student Loan	3,950.00	
Department Store	435.00	
Total Liabilities	$244,535.00	$244,535.00
Net Worth (Total Assets – Total Liabilities)		$20,165.00

At this stage, it is critical that you be completely honest with yourself about the value of your assets and make sure you have created a comprehensive list of all debts. The first time you see the amount of your net worth in black and white, you may be startled or disappointed. The idea here is not to cast you into deep despair but to see where you are today and to provide a benchmark to measure against in the future. Place a date on the statement you have just created, and be prepared to create a new statement every three to six months. You will be amazed at how quickly you can make meaningful progress when you have become committed to following the path to financial fitness.

■ ACTION 7—LAYING THE FOUNDATION FOR SUCCESS: Make a Commitment to Spend Less Than You Make

Steven K. Smartt, CFP
Managing Principal
Lincoln Financial Advisors

Professional Perspective

Steven K. Smartt has been in the financial services business for the past 25 years. Steve received a copy of *Money for Life* the day he left for a five-day business trip to San Francisco. Of his experience with the book he said, "I had it finished by the time I went to bed that night. After 25 years in the financial services business, I have come to realize that there are really just a few very basic principles that anyone who wishes to achieve financial independence must follow. *Money for Life* teaches in a very readable and understandable way the most basic, yet least-followed principle—you must spend less than you earn. Everyone will relate to at least one of the characters in the story, and by applying the principles taught in this book, everyone can achieve financial success." ■

Most of those who have amassed great wealth seem to understand a critical point with respect to money: A person will be much more successful in achieving true, long-term financial fitness if he or she focuses first on living within his or her means. The true secret lies in the way we choose to *spend* our money rather than in the way we choose to *earn* our money. Although many ways are available to earn money, only one way is available to accumulate wealth: spend less than you make! With this financial approach deeply rooted, you will be better prepared to successfully manage more money as you have opportunities to increase your income in the future. Statistically, it is very unlikely you will be able to achieve financial fitness by simply earning more money. You must first apply the principle of spending less than you make.

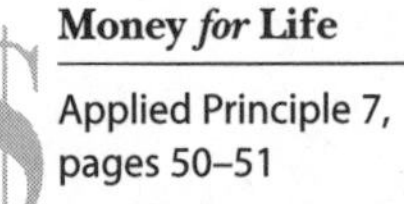

Money *for* Life
Applied Principle 7, pages 50–51

With your partner, if applicable, sign the following *Spend Less Than You Make* commitment:

Spend Less Than You Make Commitment

I, ______________________, (name) and ______________________, (partner's name, if applicable) commit to applying the principles and utilizing the tools necessary to consistently live within my/our means by spending less than I/we make.

______________________	____________
Signature	Date
______________________	____________
Signature	Date

■ ACTION 8—LAYING THE FOUNDATION FOR SUCCESS: Understand the Steps of the Success Cycle

Once you have adopted the principle of spending less than you make, you are well on your way to winning the mental financial fitness battle. After you have determined that you will take the steps necessary to become financially fit, you need to incorporate a system into your personal financial life. The Success Cycle (see Figure LF.6) is a system that can be adopted and routinely followed to ensure continued improvement and long-term financial fitness. This system includes four steps: *plan, track, compare,* and *adjust.*

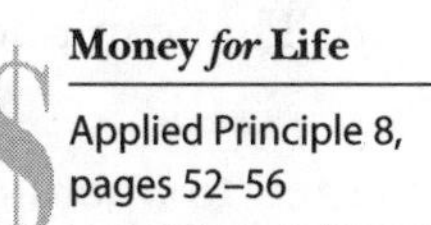
Money *for* Life
Applied Principle 8, pages 52–56

FIGURE LF.6 Success Cycle

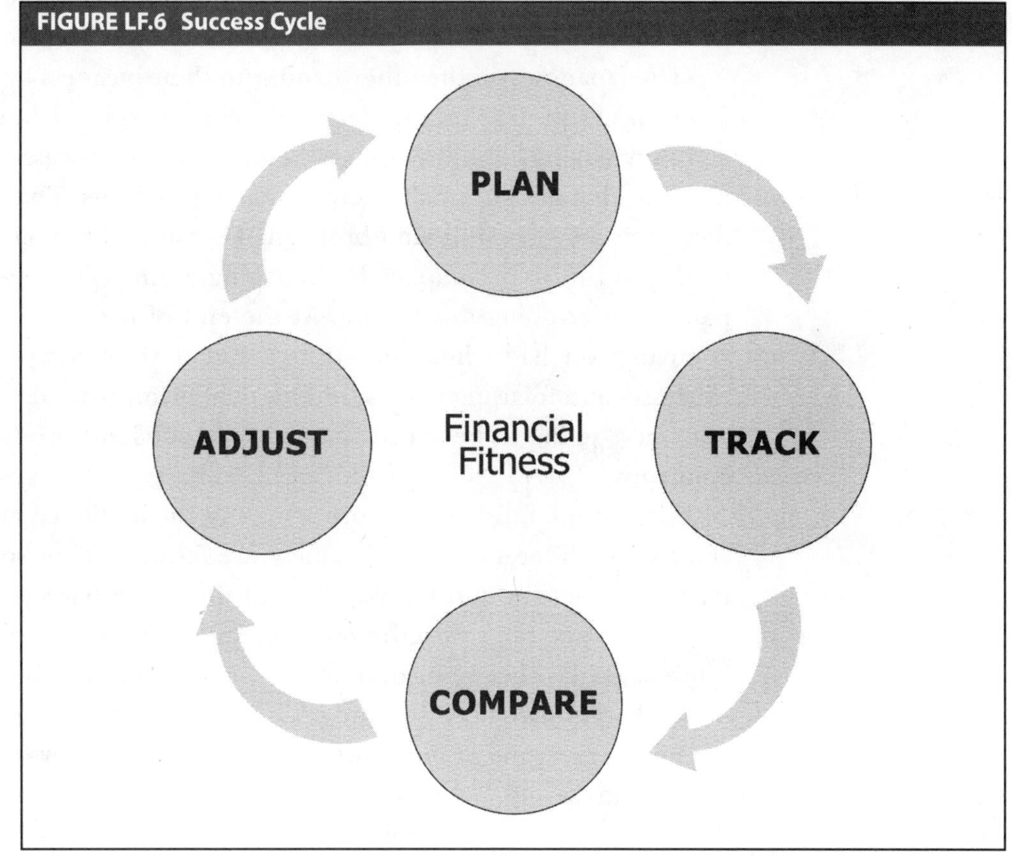

The system seems relatively simple, but results can be extraordinary when these steps are followed continuously. Successful companies everywhere incorporate this system into their monthly, quarterly, and annual management systems and processes. Successful project managers, contractors, and process management professionals all follow this cycle. What's more, the cycle can be applied to a very small project spanning a few weeks or to the construction of a multibillion-dollar industrial plant spanning a number of years. In either case, successful execution requires that each of the steps in the Success Cycle be taken. Steps cannot be shortened or eliminated. Often in our society we like to find the quick fix or the silver bullet. What we need to realize is that victory comes through the steady and persistent application of proven principles.

Some years ago, Frank Burge, a noted publisher, told a story regarding management styles in an article in the October 7, 1991, issue of *Electronic Business* magazine. His story related a conversation between himself and Alex d'Arbeloff, chairman of Teredyne. Apparently, d'Arbeloff had been trying to figure out why the Japanese were so successful. Was it, he wondered, because they're just smarter than we are? No, he thought, they're smart but no smarter than we are. Is it because they work harder? Again, they work hard, but American workers are some of the most productive, hardest-working people in the world. That can't be it either.

Then it dawned on him. He realized that most Americans tended to operate their business by managing events. When something goes wrong, we fix it. We manage to put out fires very well—what d'Arbeloff refers to as "fire-hose management"—but we fail to do anything about improving the processes that could prevent fires in the first place. Our motto usually is "If it ain't broke, don't fix it."

The Japanese, on the other hand, run their business by managing processes. They make sure that they understand the process inside and out, and then they focus on making continuous improvements in the process—not necessarily monumental changes but small, incremental adjustments. That takes patience. In effect, their motto is "If it ain't broke, make it just a little bit better."

If you run your company by managing events (putting out fires), your company is never going to improve. At the end of five years, you'll have the same company you had when you started. But if your competitor is managing its processes and focusing on continuous quality improvement over those same five years, it is going to become a much more efficient, productive, and successful company.

After Frank finished his story, a man in the audience made this observation: "Frank, the difference is the Japanese are farmers. They sow the seed. They water it. They let the sun nourish it. And then they harvest it. Farming takes patience. You just can't rush the process. Americans aren't farmers; Americans are hunters. When they want dinner, they go out and shoot something. Bang! It's done. 'Forget patience. I'm hungry.' 'Bang!'" When the gentleman finished his statement, everyone in the audience was laughing—they recognized the truth in what he was saying.

Consistent implementation of the Success Cycle forces us to become more patient—to be more like farmers and less like hunters—ensuring our long-term financial success. If you wish to correctly implement the four steps of the Success Cycle, you need to clearly understand each one.

STEP 1: Create a Plan

Without a plan, you will find it difficult, if not impossible, to find your way through the maze of personal financial complexity. Few of us would consider taking a trip to a new location without first consulting a map and planning the best travel route. So it is with financial fitness. After you have created a net-worth statement, you need to determine the direction you will take next. This includes carefully planning the way you will spend your money on a monthly basis. Planning is a process that successful companies follow meticulously. Often these plans include detailed monthly, quarterly, and annual information regarding sales, expenses, profit, and cash management.

Your monthly personal financial plan should include both a summary of the income you expect to receive during the month, and a detailed plan for spending during that month. As with all types of planning, until you have reduced the plan to writing either on paper or on the computer, it is not really a plan, only a wish. This book teaches you how to create an effective monthly plan.

STEP 2: Track Every Transaction

Once you have completed a monthly plan, you need to begin tracking your progress. Companies in America spend billions annually tracking every transaction, including sales, expenses, and cash receipts. Imagine trying to successfully manage a company without using and applying basic accounting principles. Some try, but largely they either fail or have low levels of success. This should not be surprising. Why then do so many try to achieve personal financial success without tracking their income and expenses?

Companies don't choose which transactions to track—they track *every* transaction. The only way to get complete value from tracking is to track every transaction. If you want to become financially fit, you must be prepared to carefully follow this principle. Tracking every transaction can seem overwhelming at first, but with the right tools, this can be very simple. In this book you will learn about some of these tools and how to utilize them successfully.

STEP 3: Compare Your Actual Performance with Your Plan

A written plan does little good if you don't take the next step of comparing your actual results against your plan. Again, well-managed companies utilize the comparison process on an ongoing basis. Budgetary managers in these companies receive monthly, quarterly, and annual comparison reports, which highlight the areas for review.

With physical fitness, a coach tests your performance at regular intervals and compares the new information with past results. This allows you and your coach to understand the areas in which you have improved and those areas that may require some changes.

It is the same with financial fitness. The step of comparing your actual results with your plan is a crucial one. It includes looking at both income and expenses. Planning and tracking do you very little good if you are unwilling to take time to compare your results on at least a monthly basis. As you make this comparison, you will immediately understand how and where to make necessary adjustments.

STEP 4: Make Adjustments

It is nearly impossible to create a perfect plan the first time around. Great planning is a process that includes both time and experience. As you plan, track, and compare, you are able to see clearly which areas need adjusting. These adjustments may include adding spending in some areas and reducing it in others. The entire process does you little good if, at the end of your review, you are unwilling to make necessary adjustments.

Good managers use the information provided from variance reports to make appropriate adjustments. Adjustments include changes that have an impact on both sales and expenses, ultimately enhancing the overall profitability of the enterprise. Each time you complete the cycle by making necessary adjustments, your plan becomes more accurate. You will be surprised and amazed at the adjustments you can make over time.

■ ■ ■ ■ ■

Following the Success Cycle allows you to incorporate processes followed by successful companies and project managers. What's more, the Success Cycle can be used to help you successfully achieve a number of personal goals and objectives. Other areas in which the Success Cycle could be used include physical fitness, weight loss, personal development, and educational achievement. Place a check next to each step of the Success Cycle below when you believe you understand how it can be used to help you achieve your financial fitness objectives.

1. ___ Create a plan.
2. ___ Track every transaction.
3. ___ Compare your actual performance to your plan.
4. ___ Make adjustments.

■ ACTION 9—LAYING THE FOUNDATION FOR SUCCESS: Review and Understand the Principles of Envelope Budgeting

Many have heard of, or are familiar with someone who has used, the envelope budgeting system for spending management. This system has worked exceptionally well for thousands of people in the past. Most of these people understood the basics of the system and how to use it, but many could not articulate the principles behind the system that allowed them to be successful.

The envelope system as it was used with cash was very simple. In the days before the proliferation of credit cards, debit cards, and other forms of cashless spending, many couples were dedicated to the envelope budgeting system and used it effectively for many years. Initially, a couple would sit down together and determine how much cash they would receive each month. This available cash represented the net amount of all of their paychecks for the month. Then they determined where they would be spending money. Their areas of spending included things they would purchase and pay for each and every month, as well as items they would spend money on only periodically. After completing their list, they took out a stack of envelopes and labeled one for each area of spending. Their next task was to determine the amount of money required for each envelope every month. For the areas of periodic spending, they calculated the amount they would spend each year, and then divided this amount by 12. When they had completed these tasks, the information represented their monthly spending plan.

When the couple received a paycheck, they would go to the bank and cash the check. Then they would sit together at the kitchen table and divide the cash into different envelopes based on their defined spending plan. When they paid for goods or services, they would simply spend from the specified envelope. The envelope became a self-policing spending account. Couples always knew how much money they had left to spend and how long it needed to last. Refer to Figure LF.7 for an example of how the traditional envelope method of budgeting worked.

FIGURE LF.7 Traditional Envelope Budgeting

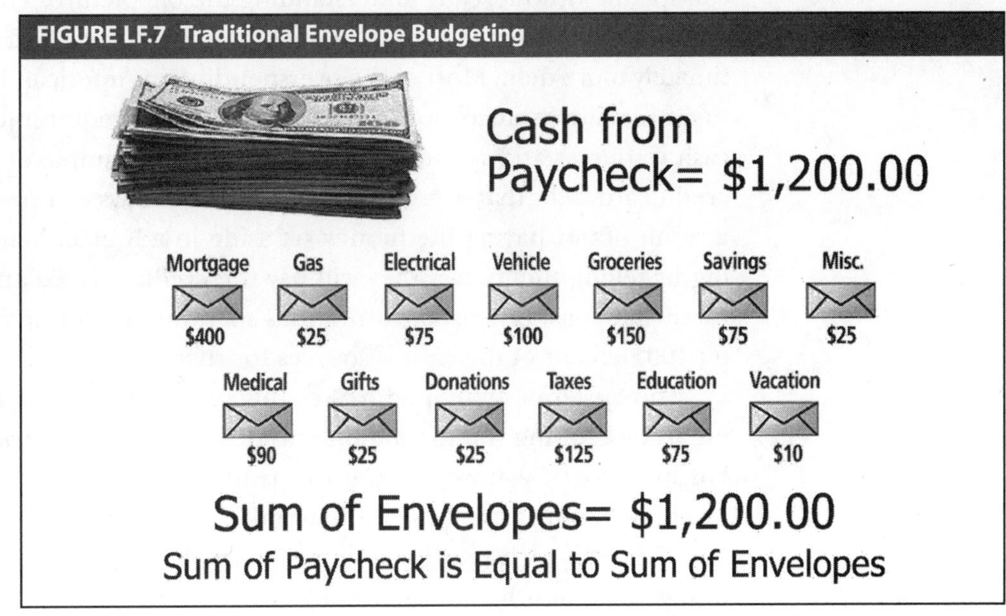

Money *for* Life

Applied Principle 9, pages 69–74

The envelope system automatically encapsulates four principles that are keys to financial success. These principles reveal the secrets of how you can achieve financial fitness by using the envelope system.

FIRST: Set Money Aside in Advance

When you commit yourself to using the envelope system, you become dedicated to living within your means. One of the primary reasons for this is that the envelope system requires you to set aside money in advance for each of the spending requirements you have. Many people in our society live paycheck to paycheck. The envelope system helps eliminate this problem because the funding for spending requirements comes from available cash resources that are allocated to categories of spending before the actual spending takes place. After following this system for just a few months, you can quickly get to the point where you have enough money set aside at the beginning of the month to meet all of that month's spending requirements.

One of the significant problems people face today is the inability to understand how future spending requirements will affect their monthly cash flow. Have you ever had an annual insurance payment surprise you? Other periodic spending requirements include vacations, property tax payments, holiday spending, gifts, auto registration fees, auto maintenance fees, house maintenance fees, furniture and appliance replacement costs, and the like. When you think about it, many things can catch us off guard if we don't plan ahead.

Most people manage their spending through their checking or savings account balance at a bank. Unfortunately, this account balance does not prepare us for the periodic spending needs that will arise in the coming months. It also doesn't alert us to the spending our partner may be planning during the next few days or weeks. So we make independent decisions about how much we think we can spend, without really understanding the big picture. This is a very dangerous approach and leads to problems, including bounced checks, frustration, and ultimately more debt. Most of the overspending in American families can be traced to an inability to incorporate periodic spending requirements into our current cash resources and spending practices. A great example of this is the amount of credit card debt that is created during the holidays or on vacations each year as a result of not having the money set aside in advance. Many justify such spending by telling themselves they will pay the credit card balance next month. This rarely happens, because next month's spending requirements are already based on 100 percent of the cash resources for that month.

The envelope system addresses this problem of periodic spending requirements by allowing you to set money aside in advance of periodic spending needs. For example, if you were going to spend $2,400 on holiday gifts each year, you would be setting aside $200 each month. To state this another way, if you want to spend $2,400 each year for holiday gifts, you need to spend $200 less on other things each month.

Perhaps your parents or grandparents used an envelope budgeting system. Imagine how they felt each December when they prepared to purchase holiday gifts and the holiday envelope was full! Imagine how you will feel when you want to take a vacation and you know that the money is already set aside in advance. Or imagine how nice it will feel to know that you have money set aside to replace the tires on your car the next time it's required. The envelope system holds the secret to setting aside money in advance.

SECOND: Spend from How Much Is Left

One of the significant secrets to not overspending is to know daily how much you have left to spend in any area of defined spending. Although this seems very simple and even obvious, consider how often you make purchases without knowing how much you can really spend before your spending outstrips your available resources—or how many times you buy something without knowing how it will negatively influence your ability to meet other spending requirements. When people used the traditional envelope system to make purchases—to buy clothes, for example—they would take the clothing envelope with them. They knew immediately how much they had left to spend and how long it had to last before they funded the envelope again. This information was invaluable in assisting them to make sound spending decisions.

If you choose to spend less than you make, then spending from what's left becomes very simple. If there isn't enough in the envelope to complete the purchase you're considering, the purchase is delayed or another purchase decision is made. Without knowing how much is left, you can only hope that the purchase decision you are about to make won't negatively impact other areas of your financial life. Unfortunately, if you don't have this critical balance information, you won't know of the negative effect until it's too late. Knowing in advance how much is left to spend is the secret to making smart and informed spending decisions every day.

THIRD: When You Run Out, You Must Make a Choice

We all want to be fully empowered to make choices. This is often one of the justifications we make for spending money. "It's my money, I've earned it, and I have the right to decide how to spend it! If I want to purchase that coat, I will, period." The problem with this thinking is that it often takes future choices away. Because you purchased that coat, you may not be able to purchase the birthday gift you wanted for your daughter.

The envelope system doesn't eliminate the ability to make personal choices; it provides information so you can make more informed decisions. With the envelope system, it is quite possible to run out of money before you fund the envelope the next time. If this happens, you have three options: (1) put off the purchase until you fund the envelope the next time; (2) purchase something less expensive; or (3) purchase the item and transfer money from another envelope to cover the cost.

All three choices still allow you to live within your means. With the third option, you can determine at the point of purchase which other area of spending you would like to impact. For example, if you wanted to purchase the coat and didn't have enough money in the clothing envelope to cover the cost, you could transfer money from your groceries envelope for the purchase. If you made this decision, you would do it with the knowledge that you would not be able to spend as much on food this month. There's nothing wrong with having made this choice. Perhaps you know that your grocery needs were less this month than in the past, or perhaps you didn't spend all the money in your grocery envelope last month so you have extra. Whatever your thinking, you have to be able to make a purchase decision and understand exactly what impact it will have in other areas of your financial life. Making a choice about a purchase is fine as long as you do it on an informed basis. The envelope system holds the secret to truly empowered purchase decision making.

FOURTH: At the End of the Period, What's Left Is Savings

One of the key principles of securing financial fitness is to save something first. In addition to setting aside a specified amount for savings each month, the envelope system allows you to save the balance remaining in many envelopes at the end of each period. For example, if you have some money left in your groceries envelope at the end of the month, you could take that money and apply it to savings, because you would be funding the envelope with enough money next month to take care of your family's needs for that period. Many of your discretionary envelope spending accounts would qualify for such a review at the end of each period.

Discretionary envelope spending accounts are envelopes covering areas of spending that are not tied to fixed expenses. Based on the spending decisions you make in such areas, you may often have money left over at the end of each period. Examples of discretionary envelope spending accounts include clothing, groceries, eating out, entertainment, and so on. By adding the amount left in each of these envelopes to your defined savings, you can significantly increase the amount you apply to savings, debt repayment, and/or long-term investments. The envelope system holds the secret to increased savings.

■ ■ ■ ■ ■

As you will be using the envelope budgeting method during your 12-week financial fitness program, make sure you understand each of the principles of envelope budgeting. Place a check next to each principle when you are comfortable with the concepts associated with it:

___ Set money aside in advance.

___ Spend from how much is left.

___ When the money runs out, you must make a choice.

___ At the end of the period, what's left is savings.

■ ACTION 10—LAYING THE FOUNDATION FOR SUCCESS: Select an Envelope Budgeting Tool

Even though people successfully used cash to implement the envelope budgeting system many years ago, it is more difficult to do so today. Many purchases can still be made conveniently with cash; however, we often pay for goods and services using checks, debit cards, credit cards, online bill payments, and even automatic withdrawals from our bank accounts. For some, the cash-based envelope system may represent the best approach for ensuring success in spending management. For others, cash may simply not be a feasible alternative, but the envelope principles are not dependent on the implementation tool used. As a result, you can successfully incorporate the envelope process using one of four basic approaches; (1) cash, (2) a paper ledger or computer spreadsheet, (3) a computer-based envelope system like Mvelopes® Personal, or (4) a combination of these.

Money *for* Life
Appendix B, pages 155–65

Selecting the appropriate implementation tool is a matter of personal taste and experience. The *Money for Life Success Planner* assists you with the implementation of either a paper ledger system or the computer-based system Mvelopes Personal. If you would like to use Mvelopes Personal but don't have a starter CD, visit http://www.mvelopes.com/moneyforlife. For more information on Mvelopes Personal, refer to Appendix A, page 109.

If you prefer to use the paper ledger system, you will find all the forms necessary for a 12-month period in Appendix B. If you are proficient with a computer spreadsheet program such as Microsoft Excel, you can create a spreadsheet to duplicate the ledgers provided in the *Success Planner.* Even if you use a paper ledger system, computer spreadsheet, or computer-based envelope system, there may be certain envelope spending accounts for which you would like to use cash. This is not a problem and can easily be done. Most people who use a combined approach use cash envelopes for many of their monthly discretionary accounts, such as groceries, entertainment, allowances, and clothing. For more information and insight into these alternatives, refer to *Money for Life,* Appendix B, page 155.

Plan and Track

■ ACTION 1—WEEK 1: Create a Spending Plan

Money *for* Life
Applied Principle 10, pages 75–84

Regardless of the approach to the envelope system that you choose, the starting point is always the same. You must first develop a spending plan. This can be done successfully by completing the following four steps.

STEP 1: Define Your Monthly Net Income

Before you can develop a detailed spending plan, you first need to know the amount of resources you have to work with. In other words, what is your net income? As most of your bills are paid on a monthly basis, you will need to calculate the amount of net income you have each month to spend from. For fixed-income sources, monthly net income can usually be calculated easily. Calculating variable income, however, can sometimes be a little tricky.

Let's start with *fixed-income sources.* Most of you receive a paycheck that represents your net pay. This net amount is what's left after taxes and employee benefits, such as insurance, have been subtracted from your gross pay. Next, you need to look at how often you receive your paycheck. If you receive one paycheck each month, your monthly income is simply the net amount of that check. If you receive a paycheck twice each month, your net monthly income is the net amount of your check multiplied by 2. If you receive a paycheck every two weeks, you multiply the amount of your paycheck by 26 (the number of paychecks you receive in a year) and then divide this amount by 12. Finally, if you receive a paycheck once each week, you multiply the net amount of your paycheck by 52 and then divide this number by 12. This monthly net income calculation is shown in Figure 1.1. Refer to Figure 1.2 to see a calculation of monthly net income from fixed-income sources. Complete the table in Figure 1.3 to determine your monthly fixed net income.

Let's move now to calculating your net income from *variable income sources,* which would include commissions, bonuses, and other sources of income that

FIGURE 1.1 Net Income Calculation

Net Income Calculation				
Frequency of Paycheck	Net Amount of Paycheck	Number of Paychecks per Year	Annual Net Income	Monthly Net Income
Every Week	$1,000.00	52	$52,000.00	$4,333.33
Every Other Week	1,000.00	26	26,000.00	2,166.67
Twice Each Month	1,000.00	24	24,000.00	2,000.00
Once Each Month	1,000.00	12	12,000.00	1,000.00
Once Each Quarter	1,000.00	4	4,000.00	333.33
Once Each Year	1,000.00	1	1,000.00	83.33

To calculate Annual Net Income, multiply the Net Amount of Paycheck by the Number of Paychecks.
To calculate Monthly Net Income, divide the Annual Net Income by 12.

FIGURE 1.2 Monthly Fixed Net Income

Monthly Net Income				
Fixed Net Income				
Income Source	Net Amount of Income	Pay Periods per Year	Annual Net Income	Monthly Net Income
Medical One	$1,772.78	26	$46,092.28	$3,841.02
Washington Elementary	1,048.34	24	25,160.16	2,096.68
Total Fixed Net Income			$71,252.44	$5,937.70

FIGURE 1.3 Fixed Net Income

Monthly Net Income				
Fixed Net Income				
Income Source	Net Amount of Income	Pay Periods per Year	Annual Net Income	Monthly Net Income
Total Fixed Net Income				

may vary in amount and frequency. Because of these variations, you need to be cautious in your approach to calculating the amount of variable income that you include in your total monthly net income.

Mvelopes® Personal Tutorial: To learn how to determine your monthly fixed income using Mvelopes Personal, click the Tutorial icon on the main toolbar and select the Income Tutorial under Setup.

If you receive a commission payment every month, you can use either the smallest monthly commission received over the past several months, or you can calculate the average amount received each month. The same is true for bonuses.

Sometimes commissions and bonuses are paid quarterly, semiannually, or even annually. In these cases, you can calculate the amount you conservatively expect to receive annually and divide this amount by 12. You must be cautious, because you will be developing a spending plan based on your monthly net income, and if this variable income represents a large percentage of your total monthly net income, you may find yourself overspending for large portions of the year.

Financially fit people whose sole source of income is variable find ways to set money aside when they receive it so that they can use it appropriately until they receive their next paycheck. Generally, these people determine their total monthly spending requirements and then use this number as their calculation of the amount of income they need to allocate to monthly spending. This way they don't spend more than they have allotted, and they have the appropriate amount of money set aside for future spending requirements.

Money *for* Life
Appendix C, pages 167–72

Refer to Figure 1.4 to see an example of calculating variable net income. Complete the table in Figure 1.5 to find your total variable net income.

FIGURE 1.4 Calculating Variable Net Income

Variable Net Income			
Income Source	Medical One Bonus		
Payment Number	Income 1	Income 2	Income 3
1	$1,099.90		
2	918.89		
3	892.65		
4	890.85		
5	840.73		
6	852.89		
7	829.94		
8	840.95		
Total	$7,166.80		
Average Check Amount	$895.85		
Lowest Check Amount	$829.94		
To calculate the Average Check Amount, divide the Total by the number of checks received.			

FIGURE 1.5 Variable Net Income

Variable Net Income						
Income Source						
Payment Number	Income 1		Income 2		Income 3	
Total						
Average Check Amount						
Lowest Check Amount						
To calculate the Average Check Amount, divide the Total by the number of checks received.						

Mvelopes® Personal Tutorial: If you are using Mvelopes Personal, click the Tutorial icon on the main toolbar, and select the Income Tutorial under Setup to learn how to determine your variable monthly net income.

Now that you have determined both your fixed and your variable monthly net income, you are prepared to calculate your total monthly net income. Refer to Figure 1.6 to see an example of calculating total monthly net income; and then complete the table in Figure 1.7 to determine your total monthly net income.

Mvelopes® Personal Tutorial: If you are using Mvelopes Personal, click the Tutorial icon on the main toolbar, and select Income Tutorial under Setup to learn how to determine your total net monthly income.

STEP 2: Define Areas of Spending (Envelope Spending Accounts)

Once you have defined your monthly net income, you are ready to define your areas of spending. For purposes of consistency, let's call these "envelope spending accounts." There are two types of envelope spending accounts—*monthly* and *periodic*. Monthly envelope spending accounts are for areas that have spending activity each month. Periodic envelope spending accounts are for areas

FIGURE 1.6 Calculating Total Monthly Net Income

Monthly Net Income				
		Fixed Net Income		
Income Source	Net Amount of Income	Pay Periods per Year	Annual Net Income	Monthly Net Income
Medical One	$1,772.78	26	$46,092.28	$3,841.02
Washington Elementary	1,048.34	24	25,160.16	2,096.68
Total Fixed Income			$71,252.44	$5,937.70
		Variable Net Income		
Income Source	Average Net Amount of Check	Pay Periods per Year	Annual Net Income	Monthly Net Income
Medical One Bonus	$895.85	4	$3,583.40	$298.62
Total Variable Net Income			$3,583.40	$298.62
Total Monthly Net Income (Fixed Net Income + Variable Net Income)				$6,236.32

FIGURE 1.7 Monthly Net Income Table

Monthly Net Income				
		Fixed Net Income		
Income Source	Net Amount of Income	Pay Periods per Year	Annual Net Income	Monthly Net Income
Total Fixed Income				
		Variable Net Income		
Income Source	Average Net Amount of Check	Pay Periods per Year	Annual Net Income	Monthly Net Income
Total Variable Net Income				
Total Monthly Net Income (Fixed Net Income + Variable Net Income)				

that have spending activity only periodically—for example, quarterly or even annually.

Let's first deal with the monthly envelope spending accounts, which can be either *required* or *discretionary*. Monthly required accounts include planned savings; car payments; and the minimum or planned payments for credit cards, mortgage payments, and the like. Monthly discretionary accounts include groceries, dining out, clothing, entertainment, allowances, and so on.

Next, let's address periodic envelope spending accounts. As with monthly accounts, these can also be split into required and discretionary spending. Periodic required accounts include items such as property taxes, periodic insurance payments, annual auto registration fees, and the like. Periodic discretionary accounts include items such as gifts, vacations, house maintenance, holiday spending, and the like.

Refer to Figure 1.8 for a sample list of envelope spending accounts, and then complete the table in Figure 1.9 by listing each of your envelope spending accounts in the appropriate sections.

Once you have completed your list of envelope spending accounts, transfer the list to the appropriate sections of the Monthly Spending Plan Worksheet in Figure 1.10.

Mvelopes® Personal Tutorial: If you are using Mvelopes Personal, click the Tutorial icon on the main toolbar, and select the Envelopes & Spending Plan Tutorial under Setup to learn how to create your envelope spending accounts.

STEP 3: Define the Amount of Monthly Spending for Each Envelope Spending Account

The next step is to determine the amount of monthly spending for each account. Starting with the list of monthly envelope spending accounts, determine an amount that represents your historical spending for each area of spending. To do this, you may have to look at past statements or receipts. For some accounts, determining this number may be a little difficult; if so, try to make a reasonable guess. Remember, after you have created your plan, you will begin tracking all expenses. After the first month, you will be able to make appropriate adjustments. Sometimes it is easier to determine the amount you spend each year. If that's the case, divide this number by 12 to determine the monthly amount.

Use the Monthly Spending Plan Worksheet to record your annual and monthly spending for each of your envelope spending accounts. As you will likely need to make adjustments, use a pencil to record this information.

Next, calculate monthly spending requirements for your periodic accounts. First, calculate the amount you will spend in each of these accounts on an annual basis. Record this number next to the appropriate envelope spending account

FIGURE 1.8 Sample List of Envelope Spending Accounts

Envelope Spending Accounts	
Monthly Envelope Spending Accounts	
Monthly Required Accounts	**Monthly Discretionary Accounts**
Mortgage	Auto Fuel
Home Equity Loan	Babysitter
Auto Loan	Clothing
American Express	Entertainment
Visa	Dining Out
Student Loan	Groceries
Savings	Haircuts
Department Store	Spending—Ryan
Music Lessons	Spending—Christine
Fitness Club	Personal Items
School Lunch	Supplies
Auto Insurance	Phone—Home
Cable	Phone—Mobile
Power	Books & Magazines
Natural Gas	
House Security	
Water, Sewer & Garbage	
Day Care	
Periodic Envelope Spending Accounts	
Periodic Required Accounts	**Periodic Discretionary Accounts**
Auto Registration	Dental Deductible
Property Tax	Doctor Visits Deductible
Homeowner's Insurance	Birthday Gifts
Life Insurance	Holiday Gifts
	Other Gifts
	Auto Maintenance
	House Maintenance
	Vacation
	Donations

FIGURE 1.9 Envelope Spending Accounts Worksheet

Envelope Spending Accounts

Monthly Envelope Spending Accounts	
Monthly Required Accounts	Monthly Discretionary Accounts

Periodic Envelope Spending Accounts	
Periodic Required Accounts	Periodic Discretionary Accounts

FIGURE 1.10 Monthly Spending Plan Worksheet

Monthly Spending Plan Month: ____________________

Monthly Envelope Spending Accounts					
Monthly Required Accounts	Annual Spending	Monthly Allocation	Monthly Discretionary Accounts	Annual Spending	Monthly Allocation
Total—Monthly Required			Total—Monthly Discretionary		

Periodic Envelope Spending Accounts					
Periodic Required Accounts	Annual Spending	Monthly Allocation	Periodic Discretionary Accounts	Annual Spending	Monthly Allocation
Total—Periodic Required			Total—Periodic Discretionary		

Spending Plan Summary		
Total Net Monthly Income		
Envelope Spending Accounts	Annual	Monthly
Total Monthly Required Spending		
Total Monthly Dsicretionary Spending		
Total Periodic Required Spending		
Total Periodic Discretionary Spending		
Total Monthly Allocations		
Balance (Net Monthly Income – Monthly Allocations)		

on the Monthly Spending Plan Worksheet. After you have completed this for each account, calculate the amount of monthly spending by dividing the annual amount by 12. Write this number next to the annual amount in the column titled "Monthly Allocation."

After you have completed this task, calculate the total monthly spending. To simplify this, you may wish to calculate the subtotals for your monthly required, monthly discretionary, periodic required, and periodic discretionary accounts. Refer to Figure 1.11 to see a sample of a monthly spending plan.

STEP 4: Balance Your Monthly Spending Plan

Now that you have determined your total monthly net income and your total monthly spending, you are prepared to balance your spending plan. A balanced monthly spending plan means your monthly spending requirements equal your total monthly net income.

Begin by determining the amount you have left after you have satisfied all of your monthly spending requirements. This number is calculated by subtracting your total monthly spending from your total monthly net income. Record your calculated monthly net income in the space provided on the Monthly Spending Plan Worksheet. Next, record the subtotals of your envelope spending accounts (monthly required, monthly discretionary, periodic required, and periodic discretionary) and then the total of all envelope spending accounts. Finally, subtract the total monthly allocations for spending from your total monthly net income.

Don't be shocked when you see this number for the first time. Most people in our society are spending about 10 percent more than they bring in each month. If you are one of the fortunate few who are spending within your monthly net income, you have a few choices. It is important that you allocate all remaining income to an envelope spending account. Income that is not allocated may be spent in ways that are haphazard and unplanned. To address this possibility, you should allocate the remaining balance to one of your envelope spending accounts, such as savings, or increase the amount you are planning for debt repayment or investments.

Most of us need to find ways to reduce the amount of our monthly allocations for spending, so that the total monthly spending is equal to the total monthly net income. The first envelope spending accounts to review are your discretionary accounts, both monthly and periodic. Review the list you have created and look for areas where you believe you can make reductions in your initial spending amounts. Keep track of the adjustments that you are making and subtract these adjustments from the total amount of overspending. Remember, the goal is to live within your means. If you really want to change your financial life, you may have to make some sacrifices. Long-term financial fitness requires dedication to this one principle: *Spend less than you make!* Thousands of people are making this choice every day, and so can you. No discretionary envelope spending account should be sacred. Making these decisions together with your partner will bring

FIGURE 1.11 Sample Monthly Spending Plan

Monthly Spending Plan — Month: September

Monthly Envelope Spending Accounts					
Monthly Required Accounts	Annual Spending	Monthly Allocation	Monthly Discretionary Accounts	Annual Spending	Monthly Allocation
Mortgage	$17,064.00	$1,422.00	Auto Fuel	$2,700.00	$225.00
Home Equity Loan	1,704.00	142.00	Babysitter	360.00	30.00
Auto Loan	6,204.00	517.00	Clothing	2,100.00	175.00
American Express	900.00	75.00	Entertainment	1,140.00	95.00
Visa	1,140.00	95.00	Dining Out	900.00	75.00
Student Loan	1,704.00	142.00	Groceries	4,800.00	400.00
Savings	3,600.00	300.00	Haircuts	420.00	35.00
Department Store	900.00	75.00	Spending—Ryan	600.00	50.00
Music Lessons	720.00	60.00	Spending—Christine	600.00	50.00
Fitness Club	360.00	30.00	Personal Items	600.00	50.00
School Lunch	240.00	20.00	Supplies	120.00	10.00
Auto Insurance	1,680.00	140.00	Phone—Home	900.00	75.00
Cable	420.00	35.00	Phone—Mobile	1,200.00	100.00
Power	1,800.00	150.00	Books & Magazines	120.00	10.00
Natural Gas	720.00	60.00			
House Security	276.00	23.00			
Water, Sewer, & Garbage	600.00	50.00			
Day Care	6,000.00	500.00			
Total—Monthly Required	$46,032.00	$3,836.00	Total—Monthly Discretionary	$16,560.00	$1,380.00

Periodic Envelope Spending Accounts					
Periodic Required Accounts	Annual Spending	Monthly Allocation	Periodic Discretionary Accounts	Annual Spending	Monthly Allocation
Auto Registration	$360.00	$30.00	Dental Deductible	$300.00	$25.00
Property Tax	1,980.00	165.00	Doctor Visits Deductible	720.00	60.00
Homeowner's Insurance	900.00	75.00	Birthday Gifts	420.00	35.00
Life Insurance	600.00	50.00	Holiday Gifts	900.00	75.00
			Other Gifts	180.00	15.00
			Auto Maintenance	1,380.00	115.00
			House Maintenance	900.00	75.00
			Vacation	2,100.00	175.00
			Donations	1,500.00	125.00
Total—Periodic Required	$3,840.00	$320.00	Total—Periodic Discretionary	$8,400.00	$700.00

Spending Plan Summary		
Total Net Monthly Income		$6,236.00
Envelope Spending Accounts	Annual	Monthly
Total Monthly Required Spending	$46,032.00	$3,836.00
Total Monthly Discretionary Spending	$16,560.00	$1,380.00
Total Periodic Required Spending	$3,840.00	$320.00
Total Periodic Discretionary Spending	$8,400.00	$700.00
Total Monthly Allocations		$6,236.00
Balance (Net Monthly Income – Monthly Allocations)		$0.00

you a greater level of success. When you are involved in the budgeting process together, you can count on successfully reaching your financial goals.

If you still have reductions to make after you have completed a review of your discretionary envelope spending accounts, you need to review your required expenses. Adjustments to these accounts are more difficult, as they usually require more significant changes. Carefully review each required envelope spending account and determine those that can be adjusted. Sometimes you can negotiate reductions in your insurance expenses or refinance existing debt to facilitate a lower interest rate, thus reducing your monthly payment. You may need to speak to certain creditors and negotiate a lower payment until you have eliminated some of your other debt and can then increase the amount you are paying.

In some cases, you may need to sell some of your assets to reduce your initial debt load. This may mean getting by with one car, selling recreational vehicles, or even downsizing your home. These are difficult choices, but if you are truly committed to becoming financially fit, you may need to make some of these adjustments. When you move forward with these adjustments to ensure a balanced monthly spending plan, you immediately feel the sense of relief that comes from knowing you are able to live within your means. If you master this principle today, tomorrow you will be able to achieve a level of financial fitness that few others enjoy. After a few short months, you will begin to reap the significant benefits of having made these choices.

Take the time to review your monthly spending plan and make the adjustments necessary to balance your plan. Record your adjustments on the Monthly Spending Plan Worksheet and recalculate the subtotals, monthly total, and balance. Once the balance is equal to zero, you have completed your balanced monthly spending plan.

Mvelopes® Personal Tutorial: If you are using Mvelopes Personal, click the Tutorial icon on the main toolbar, and select the Envelopes & Spending Plan Tutorial under Setup to learn how to complete your spending plan.

■ ACTION 2—WEEK 1: Create Envelope Spending Account Registers

Once you have defined your monthly net income, identified your envelope spending accounts, and balanced your monthly spending plan, you are prepared to create registers for each of your financial institution accounts and envelope spending accounts.

If you are using the paper ledger system, you will find a number of blank register worksheets in Appendix B, Figures B.6–B.10. These worksheets should be used to track transactions in each of your financial institution accounts as well as in your envelope spending accounts.

The first step is to prepare a register for each of your financial institution accounts, which would include any checking, savings, or credit card accounts that you will use to make purchases going forward. Let's start with your bank accounts. Look for the Bank Account Register Worksheet in Appendix B, Figure B.6. Write the name of the bank account on the top of the worksheet in the space provided. Next, determine the beginning balance of this account by looking at the last statement for the account or the current online balance. If you are using your last statement, write the statement date in the opening field of the date column on the register worksheet. If you are using an online balance, record the date that you retrieved the online balance. Next, write "Beginning Balance" in the first line of the "Transaction Description" column. Finally, write the current balance amount in the first line of the "Balance" column. Repeat this for each checking account and savings account you wish to use with your envelope spending management system. Remember, you can use any number of accounts; it is generally easier, however, with fewer accounts to track. See Figure 1.12 for an example of a checking account register with the beginning balance recorded.

After you have finished preparing the registers for your checking and savings accounts, prepare a register worksheet for each credit card you plan to use with your envelope spending management system. You will also find a Credit Card Account Register Worksheet in Appendix B, Figure B.9. Follow the directions above to prepare registers for the credit card accounts you plan to use going forward. See Figure 1.13 for an example of a credit card register with the beginning balance recorded.

Most people use cash to purchase certain goods and services; therefore, if you plan to use cash going forward, you should prepare a cash register to track these transactions. Again, you will find a Cash Account Register Worksheet in Appendix B, Figure B.8. Determine the amount of cash you have on hand and enter this amount as the beginning balance. Also record the date of the beginning balance. See Figure 1.14 for an example of a cash account register with the beginning balance recorded.

FIGURE 1.12 Checking Account Register with a Beginning Balance

Bank Account Register — Bank Account: *Checking Account*

Date	Transaction ID Number	Transaction Description	Deposit +	Expense –	Cleared	Balance
09/01		Beginning Balance				$1,532.00

FIGURE 1.13 Credit Card Register with a Beginning Balance

Credit Card Account Register — Credit Card Account: Visa Card

Date	Transaction ID Number	Transaction Description	Deposit +	Expense –	Cleared	Balance
09/01		Beginning Balance				–$4,350.00

FIGURE 1.14 Cash Account Register with a Beginning Balance

Cash Account Register — Cash Account: Cash

Date	Transaction Description	Deposit +	Expense –	Balance
09/01	Beginning Balance			$125.00

Next, let's prepare each of your envelope spending account registers. The Envelope Spending Account Register Worksheets are also located in Appendix B, Figure B.7. You will need to prepare one register for each of the envelope spending accounts you identified on your spending plan. Write the name of the envelope spending account at the top of the register worksheet and record the beginning balance of zero. Once you have completed this for each of your envelope spending accounts, you are ready to move on. See Figure 1.15 for an example of an envelope spending account register with a zero beginning balance.

FIGURE 1.15 Envelope Spending Account Register with a Beginning Balance of Zero

Envelope Spending Account Register — Spending Account: *Clothing*

Date	Transaction ID Number	Transaction Description	Deposit +	Expense –	Balance
09/01		*Beginning Balance*			*$0.00*

Mvelopes® Personal Tutorial: If you are using Mvelopes Personal, you have already set up a register for each envelope spending account by simply creating the account. Refer now to the section of the tutorial where you will learn about adding your financial institution accounts. In Mvelopes Personal, click the Tutorial icon on the main toolbar, and select the Bank and Credit Card Accounts Tutorial under Setup.

■ ACTION 3—WEEK 1: Create Beginning Balances for Your Envelope Spending Accounts

Money *for* Life

Appendix B, pages 155–65

You are now prepared to allocate the amount of money you have on hand to your envelope spending accounts. Remember that with the envelope system, the amount of money you have on hand should be equal to the sum of the money in each of your envelope spending accounts. If you are using a cash-based envelope system, you simply place the cash on hand in the appropriate envelope. With a paper ledger or computer system, you need to allocate the money you have on hand to the appropriate envelope spending account registers.

Next, you need to determine the total amount of money you have available. This is done by calculating the total current balance in each of your checking and savings accounts that you wish to use with the envelope budgeting system. You also need to include in this total any cash that you have recorded on your cash account register. Once you have determined the total available money, you need to allocate the entire amount among your envelope spending accounts. Normally, this is done based on the priority of required payments to be made. For example, if you have a car payment due within a few days, you may wish to allocate the available cash to that envelope spending account.

By referring to the example in Figure 1.16, complete the worksheet in Figure 1.17 to determine how to allocate your money on hand.

FIGURE 1.16 Initial Allocation for Envelope Spending Accounts

Initial Allocation—Beginning Balance for Envelope Spending Accounts

Monthly Envelope Spending Accounts — Date: 9/01

Monthly Required Accounts	Beginning Balance	Monthly Discretionary Accounts	Beginning Balance
Mortgage	$0.00	Auto Fuel	$69.00
Home Equity Loan	0.00	Babysitter	20.00
Auto Loan	0.00	Clothing	50.00
American Express	75.00	Entertainment	20.00
Visa	95.00	Dining Out	30.00
Student Loan	0.00	Groceries	200.00
Savings	0.00	Haircuts	0.00
Department Store	0.00	Spending—Ryan	0.00
Music Lessons	60.00	Spending—Christine	0.00
Fitness Club	0.00	Personal Items	0.00
School Lunch	0.00	Supplies	30.00
Auto Insurance	140.00	Phone—Home	50.00
Cable	35.00	Phone—Mobile	0.00
Power	150.00	Books & Magazines	0.00
Natural Gas	60.00		
House Security	23.00		
Water, Sewer & Garbage	50.00		
Day Care	500.00		

Periodic Envelope Spending Accounts

Periodic Required Accounts	Beginning Balance	Periodic Discretionary Accounts	Beginning Balance
Auto Registration	$0.00	Dental Deductible	$0.00
Property Tax	0.00	Doctor Visits Deductible	0.00
Homeowner's Insurance	0.00	Birthday Gifts	0.00
Life Insurance	0.00	Holiday Gifts	0.00
		Other Gifts	0.00
		Auto Maintenance	0.00
		House Maintenance	0.00
		Vacation	0.00
		Donations	0.00

Total Balance of Accounts (Bank Account and Actual Cash on Hand)	$1,657.00
Total Allocated to Envelope Spending Accounts	$1,657.00
Balance (Total Balance of Accounts – Total Allocated to Envelope Spending Accounts)	$0.00

FIGURE 1.17 Initial Allocation Worksheet—Beginning Balance for Envelope Spending Accounts

Initial Allocation—Beginning Balance for Envelope Spending Accounts

Monthly Envelope Spending Accounts — Date: 9/01

Monthly Required Accounts	Beginning Balance	Monthly Discretionary Accounts	Beginning Balance

Periodic Envelope Spending Accounts

Periodic Required Accounts	Beginning Balance	Periodic Discretionary Accounts	Beginning Balance

Total Balance of Accounts (Bank Account and Actual Cash on Hand)	
Total Allocated to Envelope Spending Accounts	
Balance (Total Balance of Accounts – Total Allocated to Envelope Spending Accounts)	

Next, completely allocate the entire amount of money on hand by recording deposit transactions on the appropriate envelope spending account registers based on your Initial Allocation Worksheet. Include the date and the description (i.e., "initial allocation") on the registers you have prepared from the blank envelope spending account register forms. Remember, when you are finished, the combined balance of your envelope spending accounts should equal the combined total of all money on hand, including the balances of your bank accounts. Refer to the example in Figure 1.18 to see how initial cash on hand is appropriately allocated and recorded on each envelope spending account register.

Mvelopes® Personal Tutorial: If you are using Mvelopes Personal, click the Tutorial icon on the main toolbar, and select the Bank and Credit Card Accounts & Assign Balances Tutorial under Setup to learn how to allocate initial cash on hand.

FIGURE 1.18 Initial Deposit/Allocation Transactions on Paper Ledgers

Envelope Spending Account Register — Spending Account: Auto Insurance

Date	Transaction ID Number	Transaction Description	Deposit +	Expense –	Balance
09/01		Beginning Balance			$0.00
09/01		Initial Allocation	$140.00		$140.00

Envelope Spending Account Register — Spending Account: Cable

Date	Transaction ID Number	Transaction Description	Deposit +	Expense –	Balance
09/01		Beginning Balance			$0.00
09/01		Initial Allocation	$35.00		$35.00

Envelope Spending Account Register — Spending Account: Power

Date	Transaction ID Number	Transaction Description	Deposit +	Expense –	Balance
09/01		Beginning Balance			$0.00
09/01		Initial Allocation	$150.00		$150.00

Envelope Spending Account Register — Spending Account: Groceries

Date	Transaction ID Number	Transaction Description	Deposit +	Expense –	Balance
09/01		Beginning Balance			$0.00
09/01		Initial Allocation	$200.00		$200.00

■ ACTION 4—WEEK 1: Create a Monthly Income Allocation Plan

Money *for* Life

Appendix B, pages 155–65, and Appendix C, pages 167–72

Your monthly income allocation plan provides a map for the allocation of your income as you receive it throughout the month. Each time you receive income, you will need to record it as a deposit on the appropriate bank account register. You then need to allocate that income to one, or several, of your envelope spending accounts. The monthly income allocation plan assists you in determining which income should be allocated to which envelope spending account.

If you are using the paper ledger system, you will need to complete the Monthly Income Allocation Plan Worksheet, which can be found in Appendix B, Figure B.12. To complete this form, list each of your envelope spending accounts in the appropriate section of the first column. In the next column, include the monthly allocation amount from your monthly spending plan. In each of the following columns, record each paycheck you will receive during the month at the top of the column in the space titled "Amount of Income." Be sure to also fill in the income source and date received, so that all income is accounted for. Next, allocate the complete amount of each paycheck to the appropriate envelope spending accounts based on the priority you wish to set and the amount you have determined you will spend. Repeat this for each check you will receive throughout the month. Make sure the total allocation at the bottom of the column is equal to the amount of income recorded at the top of the column. Refer to Figure 1.19 for an example of how this worksheet should be completed.

Money *for* Life

Appendix C, pages 167–72

If your income is primarily variable in nature, you may need to allocate a portion of your savings, or funds from an income-holding account, in order to meet your spending requirements for the month. If this is the case, use savings as one of the income sources and complete the Monthly Income Allocation Plan Worksheet as indicated.

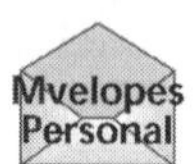

Mvelopes® Personal Tutorial: If you are using Mvelopes Personal, click the Tutorial icon on the main toolbar, and select the Funding Plan and Profiles Tutorial under Setup to learn how to create your funding plan and income profiles.

■ ACTION 5—WEEK 1: Properly Track All Transactions

Money *for* Life

Appendix B, pages 155–65 and Appendix C, pages 167–72

Money *for* Life

Applied Principle 11, pages 105–6

You are now ready to begin using your selected envelope budgeting tool. You have created a monthly spending plan, identified envelope spending accounts, prepared bank account registers and envelope spending account registers, allocated initial cash on hand, and defined your monthly income allocation plan. Your task now is to follow the plan you have set, which moves you to the *tracking* phase of the Success Cycle.

To successfully measure your progress, you must be prepared to track every transaction. Tracking every transaction can seem daunting at first, but with the help of the right tools, this task can become simple, even automatic. The most

FIGURE 1.19 Sample Monthly Income Allocation Plan

Monthly Allocation Plan					Month:	September	
	Income Source	Medical One	Wash. Elem.	Medical One	Wash. Elem.	Medical One Bonus	Medical One
	Date of Receipt	09-03	09-15	09-17	09-30	Quarterly	Check 25 & 26
	Amount of Income	$1,772.78	$1,048.34	$1,772.78	$1,048.33	Yet to Be Received	Yet to Be Received
Envelope Spending Accounts	Monthly Required Allocation	Allocation Amount	Allocation Amount	Allocation Amount	Allocation Amount	Allocation Amount	Allocation Amount
Monthly Required							
Mortgage	$1,422.00	$1,422.00					
Home Equity Loan	142.00	142.00					
Auto Loan	517.00	208.78	$308.22				
American Express	75.00		75.00				
Visa	95.00		95.00				
Student Loan	142.00		142.00				
Savings	300.00		300.00				
Department Store	75.00		75.00				
Music Lessons	60.00		53.12	$6.88			
Fitness Club	30.00			30.00			
School Lunch	20.00			20.00			
Auto Insurance	140.00			140.00			
Cable	35.00			35.00			
Power	150.00			150.00			
Natural Gas	60.00			60.00			
House Security	23.00			23.00			
Water, Sewer & Garbage	50.00			50.00			
Day Care	500.00			500.00			
Monthly Discretionary							
Auto Fuel	$225.00			$225.00			
Babysitter	30.00			30.00			
Clothing	175.00			175.00			
Entertainment	95.00			95.00			
Dining Out	75.00			75.00			
Groceries	400.00			157.90	$242.10		
Haircuts	35.00				35.00		
Spending—Ryan	50.00				50.00		
Spending—Christine	50.00				50.00		
Personal Items	50.00				50.00		
Supplies	10.00				10.00		
Phone—Home	75.00				75.00		
Phone—Mobile	100.00				100.00		
Books & Magazines	10.00				10.00		
Periodic Required							
Auto Registration	$30.00				$30.00		
Property Tax	165.00				165.00		
Homeowner's Insurance	75.00				75.00		
Life Insurance	50.00				50.00		
Periodic Discretionary							
Dental Deductible	$25.00				$25.00		
Doctor Visits Deductible	60.00				60.00		
Birthday Gifts	35.00				21.23		
Holiday Gifts	75.00						
Other Gifts	15.00						
Auto Maintenance	115.00						
House Maintenance	75.00						
Vacation	175.00						
Donations	125.00						
Total Allocations:	$6,236.00	$1,772.78	$1,048.34	$1,772.78	$1,048.33		

critical component of successful tracking is the proactive decision to do it. Once you have made this decision, implementation becomes much easier.

Let's first address tracking income transactions or deposits to your bank accounts. If you are using the paper ledger system, follow the monthly allocation plan that you have created. As you receive a deposit into one of your bank accounts, record it on the bank account register you prepared for that account. Next, refer to your monthly income allocation plan to determine how that income deposit should be allocated among your envelope spending accounts. Properly record the amount shown in your allocation plan on each of the appropriate envelope spending account registers. Refer to Figure 1.20 to see an example of how an income deposit should be allocated to envelope spending accounts.

Mvelopes® Personal Tutorial: If you are using Mvelopes Personal, click the Tutorial icon on the main toolbar, and select the Assign a Deposit Transaction Tutorial under Transactions to assign a deposit transaction to an income profile.

FIGURE 1.20 Recording an Income Deposit on a Bank Register and a Spending Account Register

Bank Account Register — Banking Account: Checking Account

Date	Transaction ID Number	Transaction Description	Deposit +	Expense –	Cleared	Balance
09/01		Beginning Balance				$1,532.00
09/03		Medical One—Payroll Deposit	$1,772.78			3,304.78

When a check is deposited, it is allocated according to the *Monthly Income Allocation Plan.* $1,422.00 is allocated to the Mortgage envelope.

Envelope Spending Account Register — Spending Account: Mortgage

Date	Transaction ID Number	Transaction Description	Deposit +	Expense –	Balance
09/01		Beginning Balance			$0.00
09/03		Monthly Allocation	$1,422.00		1,422.00

Next, let's address tracking expense transactions. If you are using the paper ledger system, you need to manually record each expense transaction as it occurs. The first step is to record the transaction on the appropriate bank account register. Write the date of the transaction in the date field and record a description in the transaction description field. Next, write the amount of the transaction in the expense field. Finally, calculate the new balance and record the updated balance in the balance field. See Figure 1.21 for an example of recording an expense transaction on a bank account register.

Next, you need to record the transaction on the appropriate envelope spending account register. Find the desired envelope spending account register and record the transaction in the same fashion as you did with the bank account register. Finish by updating the balance of the envelope spending account. See Figure 1.22 for an example of recording an expense transaction on an envelope spending account register.

Mvelopes® Personal Tutorial: If you are using Mvelopes Personal, click the Tutorial icon on the main toolbar, and select the Assign a Payment Transaction Tutorial under Transactions to learn how to assign expense transactions.

Money *for* Life
Appendix B, page 161

At times you will make a payment for goods or services that relates to two or more envelope spending accounts. An example of this would be purchasing food and an article of clothing in the same transaction. In this case, you will need to record the total transaction amount on the appropriate bank account register and then split the transaction accordingly between your grocery and your clothing envelope spending account registers.

Refer to Figure 1.23 to see how to record a split transaction if you are using the paper ledger envelope system.

FIGURE 1.21 Expense Transaction on a Bank Account Register

Bank Account Register — Bank Account: Checking Account

Date	Transaction ID Number	Transaction Description	Deposit +	Expense –	Cleared	Balance
09/01		Beginning Balance				$1,532.00
09/03		Medical One—Payroll Deposit	$1,772.78			3,304.78
09/05	Check #419	Countrywide Home Loans		$1,422.00		1,882.78

FIGURE 1.22 Expense Transaction on a Spending Account Register

Envelope Spending Account Register — Spending Account: Mortgage

Date	Transaction ID Number	Transaction Description	Deposit +	Expense –	Balance
09/01		Beginning Balance			$0.00
09/03		Monthly Allocation	$1,422.00		1,422.00
09/05	Check #419	Countrywide Home Loans		$1,422.00	0.00

Mvelopes® Personal Tutorial: If you are using Mvelopes Personal, click the Tutorial icon on the main toolbar, and select the Split a Payment Transaction Tutorial under Transactions to learn how to split a payment transaction.

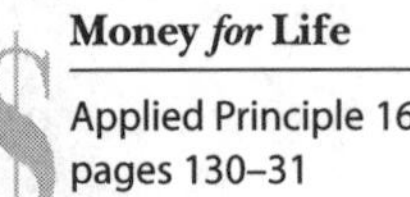

Money *for* Life

Applied Principle 16, pages 130–31

Credit cards have become such a major part of our society that many purchases can be made only with a credit card or debit card. In the United States, only about one-third of those who have credit cards pay their balance in full each month; the other two-thirds carry a balance from one month to the next. The interest rate associated with the outstanding balance generally averages about 12 percent and can sometimes exceed 25 percent. Credit cards represent a major convenience for many people but also have become a significant burden for most.

One of the biggest problems with credit card spending is that most people don't incorporate these purchases into their available monthly cash flow. As a result, purchases are often made that exceed an individual's monthly net income. Most people intend to pay the balance each month, but as the month rolls forward, they don't have the resources necessary to pay the balance. Because of the inherent problems and financial risks associated with credit card spending, many financial advisors and coaches suggest their clients not use credit cards at all. If you need a card to pay for a hotel visit, rental car, or flight purchase, the safest card to use is a debit card, because the purchase is made from existing funds in your bank account.

If you are intent on making purchases with a credit card, the envelope system provides a method for using credit cards appropriately. The key to successful credit card spending is making sure you set aside an amount of money from your monthly net income equal to your credit card purchases, thus ensuring you can pay the card balance in full each month. Every time you make a purchase with a credit card, take money from the appropriate envelope and place it in the credit card repay-

FIGURE 1.23 Recording a Split Transaction

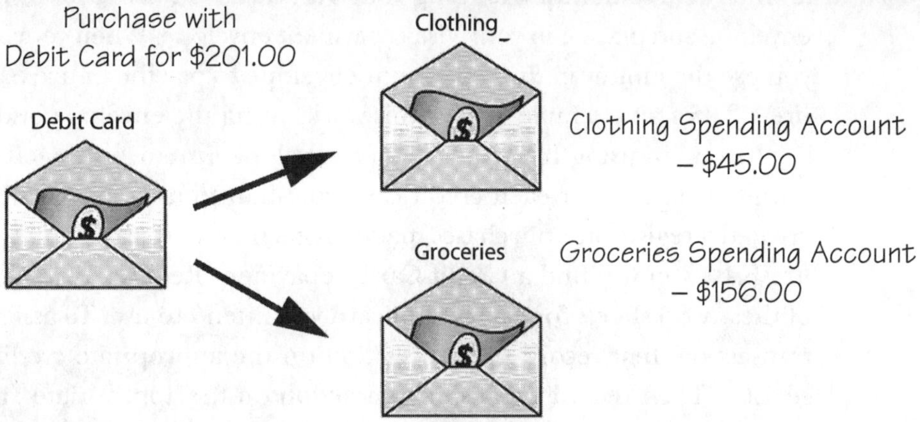

Purchase with
Debit Card for $201.00

Debit Card

Clothing

Clothing Spending Account
– $45.00

Groceries

Groceries Spending Account
– $156.00

Bank Account Register — Bank Account: Checking Account

Date	Transaction ID Number	Transaction Description	Deposit +	Expense –	Cleared	Balance
09/01		Beginning Balance				$1,532.00
09/03		Medical One—Payroll Deposit	$1,772.78			3,304.78
09/05	Check #419	Countrywide Home Loans		$1,422.00		1,882.78
09/08	Debit Card	Target—Clothing & Groceries (split)		201.00		1,681.78

Envelope Spending Account Register — Spending Account: Clothing

Date	Transaction ID Number	Transaction Description	Deposit +	Expense –	Balance
09/01		Beginning Balance			$0.00
09/01		Initial Allocation	$50.00		50.00
09/08	Debit Card	Target—Clothing Purchase (Split)		$45.00	5.00

Envelope Spending Account Register — Spending Account: Groceries

Date	Transaction ID Number	Transaction Description	Deposit +	Expense –	Balance
09/01		Beginning Balance			$0.00
09/01		Initial Allocation	$200.00		200.00
09/08	Debit Card	Target—Grocery Purchase (Split)		$156.00	44.00

ment envelope. For example, if you want to purchase an article of clothing from an Internet retailer for $45 using your Visa card, you take $45 from your clothing envelope and place it in your Visa repayment envelope. When your Visa bill arrives, you use the money in the repayment envelope to pay the entire balance. See Figure 1.24 for an example of how this works using the envelope budgeting system.

If you are using the paper ledger envelope system, you need to create a repayment register for each credit card you plan to use. You should have already created a register for purchases made on each of these cards. In Appendix B, Figure B.10, you will find a Credit Card Repayment Register Worksheet. Label one of these worksheets for each credit card you intend to use. To assign a credit card transaction, first record the transaction on the appropriate credit card account register. Then record a transfer transaction on the appropriate envelope spending account register or registers. Finally, record a deposit transaction on the appropriate credit card repayment register. See Figure 1.25 for an example of how to record a credit card purchase.

When you make a credit card payment, first record an expense transaction on the appropriate bank account register—the account from which the credit card payment was made. Next, record the payment as a deposit on the credit card account register. Finally, record the payment as an expense on the credit card repayment register. See Figure 1.26 for an example of how to record a credit card payment.

Mvelopes
Personal

Mvelopes® Personal Tutorial: If you are using Mvelopes Personal, the assignment to the credit card repayment account envelope is handled automatically when you assign an Expense transaction from a credit card account. For information on how to assign a credit card payment transaction, click Tutorial on the main toolbar and open Transactions. Select Assigning a Credit Card Payment Transaction.

Check and date below when you have completed tracking all transactions for this first week:

Check ________ Date ____________________

FIGURE 1.24 Credit Card Repayment

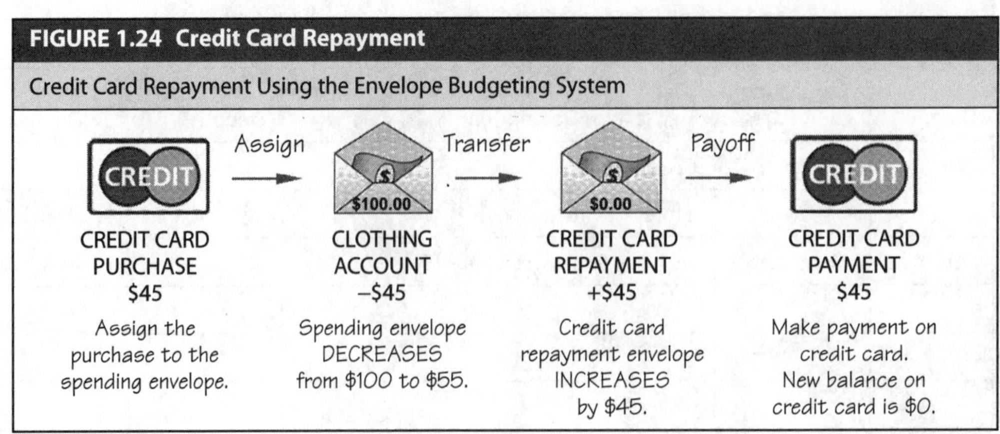
Credit Card Repayment Using the Envelope Budgeting System
CREDIT
Assign
$100.00
Transfer
$0.00
Payoff
CREDIT
CREDIT CARD PURCHASE $45
Assign the purchase to the spending envelope.
CLOTHING ACCOUNT –$45
Spending envelope DECREASES from $100 to $55.
CREDIT CARD REPAYMENT +$45
Credit card repayment envelope INCREASES by $45.
CREDIT CARD PAYMENT $45
Make payment on credit card. New balance on credit card is $0.

FIGURE 1.25 Credit Card Transaction—Purchase

Credit Card Account Register — Credit Card Account: American Express

Date	Transaction ID Number	Transaction Description	Deposit +	Expense –	Cleared	Balance
09/01		Beginning Balance				–$4,855.00
09/09	Trans #568	CostCo—Groceries		$44.00		–4,899.00

When a purchase is made with a credit card, that amount is deducted from the envelope spending account and recorded on the credit card register.

Envelope Spending Account Register — Spending Account: Groceries

Date	Transaction ID Number	Transaction Description	Deposit +	Expense –	Balance
09/01		Beginning Balance			$0.00
09/01		Initial Allocation	$200.00		200.00
09/08	Debit Card	Target—Grocery Purchase (Split)		$156.00	44.00
09/09	Trans #568	CostCo—Groceries (AMEX)		44.00	0.00

After recording the transaction on the envelope spending account register, you will also record the purchase as a deposit to your credit card repayment register. You will then have the money already set aside for payment later in the month.

Credit Card Repayment Register — Credit Card Account: American Express

Date	Transaction ID Number	Transaction Description	Deposit +	Expense –	Balance
09/01		Initial Allocation	$75.00		$75.00
09/09	Trans #568	CostCo—Groceries	44.00		119.00

FIGURE 1.26 Credit Card Transaction—Payment

Bank Account Register

Bank Account: Checking Account

Date	Transaction ID Number	Transaction Description	Deposit +	Expense –	Cleared	Balance
09/01		Beginning Balance				$1,532.00
09/03		Medical One—Payroll Deposit	$1,772.78			3,304.78
09/05	Check #419	Countrywide Home Loans		$1,422.00		1,882.78
09/08	Debit Card	Target—Clothing & Groceries (split)		201.00		1,621.78
09/20	Check #420	American Exp. Card Payment		194.00		1,427.78

When it's time to pay the credit card bill, the money is already set aside for the payment. Simply write a check from your bank account and fill in the transaction on the credit card register and the credit card repayment register.

Credit Card Account Register

Credit Card Account: American Express

Date	Transaction ID Number	Transaction Description	Deposit +	Expense –	Cleared	Balance
09/01		Beginning Balance				–$4,855.00
09/09	Trans #568	CostCo—Groceries		$44.00		–4,899.00
09/20	Check #420	AMEX Payment—From Checking	$194.00			–4,705.00

Credit Card Repayment Register

Credit Card Account: American Express

Date	Transaction ID Number	Transaction Description	Deposit +	Expense –	Balance
09/01		Initial Allocation	$75.00		$75.00
09/09	Trans #568	CostCo—Groceries	44.00		119.00
09/15		Monthly Allocation	75.00		194.00
09/20	Check #420	AMEX Payment—From Checking		$194.00	0.00

■ ACTION 6—WEEK 1: Use Your Envelope Budgeting Tool to Make Appropriate Spending Decisions During the Week

Money *for* Life

Applied Principle 12, pages 107–8

One of the most often cited objections to the idea of budgeting is the thought that budgets become restrictive and frustrating. The feeling that you can't make purchases when you want to can be very disconcerting for many people. In reality, however, as you spend beyond your income resources, your spending choices become increasingly more restricted. Real, long-lasting choice comes from making the decision to live within your means.

That said, there are many times when deciding to spend beyond your current resources in a specific envelope spending account is just fine. Let's say that you would like to purchase an article of clothing for $100 but have only $79 in the clothing envelope spending account. In this case, you have to decide if you would like to put off the purchase until you have more money in the clothing envelope, purchase a less expensive item of clothing, or transfer money from another envelope spending account to cover the added cost, therefore necessitating reduced spending in that category. As you can see, the information provided with the envelope system has truly empowered you to make an informed decision.

Making a decision to transfer money from another envelope is not a problem, because you have made a decision to spend less in that other area. For example, let's say you have $250 in your groceries envelope spending account and decide to transfer $25 into the clothing envelope spending account to cover the added cost of the clothing purchase mentioned above. If you are using the paper ledger budgeting system, you need to show that you have transferred money from the groceries envelope spending account to the clothing account. See Figure 1.27 for an example of how a transfer is recorded on your envelope spending account registers.

Mvelopes® Personal Tutorial: If you are using Mvelopes Personal, click the Tutorial icon on the main toolbar, and select the Transfer Money Between Envelopes Tutorial under Other Tutorials to learn how to transfer money from one envelope to another.

Now let's say that you did not have the extra money in another envelope to transfer to the clothing envelope. If you are dedicated to living within your means, your only option is to either purchase a less expensive item or wait until you have more money in the clothing envelope. Choosing to spend the extra $25 when the resources are not available limits your choices in the future, because you have just created debt by spending above and beyond your monthly net income resources. This means you will be paying more interest next month and further reducing available resources to purchase the things you want or, more important, need.

FIGURE 1.27 Envelope Spending Account Transfer

Envelope Spending Account Register — Spending Account: *Groceries*

Date	Transaction ID Number	Transaction Description	Deposit +	Expense –	Balance
09/17		Balance Forward			$250.00
09/17		Envelope Transfer to Clothing		$25.00	225.00

If you need to make a clothing purchase and there is not enough money in your envelope spending account, you can easily transfer from another account. Enter the transaction on the registers for both accounts.

Envelope Spending Account Register — Spending Account: *Clothing*

Date	Transaction ID Number	Transaction Description	Deposit +	Expense –	Balance
09/17		Balance Forward			$79.00
09/17		Envelope Transfer from Groceries	$25.00		104.00

Your chosen envelope tool assists you with making appropriate and informed spending decisions by providing critical information about the remaining balance in each envelope spending account. However, your ability to live within your means on a daily basis depends on your commitment to making purchase decisions based on this information.

Check and date below when you have made all purchase decisions for this first week by following the balance information provided by your envelope budgeting tool:

Check ________ Date ____________________

Track

Success Story

Meet the Lunt family. Rick is a teacher at the elementary school in their Spanish Fork, Utah, neighborhood. Melissa doesn't work outside the home but has her hands full with three small children.

The Lunts' situation is one that rings true for many young families—living paycheck to paycheck with the expenses of three small children and only one income. With their consumer debt, not including auto loans, accumulating closer and closer to $13,000, they were worried about paying the monthly bills and taking care of their family's needs. When Melissa was introduced to the envelope method of budgeting, she knew it would be a big help. She decided to use a computer-based envelope system because she knew the program would save her time and money.

After less than a year of adopting the envelope budgeting principles and using the computer-based envelope method, the Lunts were able to pay off their entire $8,000 credit card balance and $1,500 in outstanding medical bills. That's nearly an extra $900 per month that was recovered from hidden spending! They are now less than four months from being free of consumer debt.

Melissa loves the system and has fun balancing the accounts and paying the bills instead of worrying about them every single month. She states: "I love it! My favorite part, of course, is watching that debt account go down each and every month! Because of the savings within our envelope spending accounts, our bank account balance now stays way over $1,000. I'm looking forward to it continuing to grow. Goodbye to the days when we were running to the bank to make a deposit because our balance was going to be in the negative. What freedom! Our life will never be the same. We have been using the envelope budgeting approach for about a year now and will never use anything else again." ■

Now that you have completed the first week, you are well on your way to becoming financially fit. And like the Lunt family, you too will experience the joy and satisfaction of living within your means and significantly reducing your debt.

By now, you have developed your monthly spending plan and have begun to track your spending by using your selected envelope budgeting tool; you can move on to week 2 with confidence. During this week, you will continue to track your transactions and make appropriate spending decisions based on the envelope spending account balance information now available to you.

Check and date each of the following actions when you have completed them for the week.

■ ACTION 1—WEEK 2: Record All Deposits *(See Action 5, Week 1, page 46.)*

Record all deposits on your bank account registers and appropriately allocate them to your envelope spending accounts according to your monthly income allocation plan. Record the appropriate amount on each of your account registers.

Check ________ Date ____________________

■ ACTION 2—WEEK 2: Track All Expenses *(See Action 5, Week 1, page 46.)*

Track all expense transactions for the week by recording them on the appropriate bank account register and envelope spending account registers.

Check ________ Date ____________________

■ ACTION 3—WEEK 2: Track All Credit Card Transactions *(See Action 5, Week 1, page 46.)*

Track all credit card transactions for the week by recording them on the appropriate credit card account register, envelope spending account registers, and credit card repayment register.

Check ________ Date ____________________

■ ACTION 4—WEEK 2: Check Balances *(See Action 6, Week 1, page 55.)*

Make appropriate spending decisions by spending from the balance remaining in your envelope spending accounts. Make any transfers between envelope spending accounts that are appropriate.

Check ________ Date ____________________

Congratulations, you are now ready for week 3!

Track

Success Story

Have you ever heard the saying "The more you make, the more you spend"? Rob and Colleen Joseph experienced that firsthand! As Rob's salary continued to increase, they just kept spending more. Like so many in their situation, the Josephs soon found themselves with a rather large amount of debt, never knowing where the money was disappearing to. Every year Rob thought, "This is the year that we will get ahead!" But they never got ahead; in fact, they did just the opposite—falling deeper and deeper into debt.

When Rob lost his job in 2001, during one of the biggest economic downturns in recent history, of course the family was concerned, stressed, and worried about how to make ends meet. While Rob was looking for work, he would review their financial situation in disgust and frustration. How could they have been overspending by so much? "I mean, sure. This sounds like an overweight person wondering if maybe overeating could be part of the problem. Obviously, I get that," Rob remarked. "But if a financial management system is to be of any help, it has to help you change your spending habits. A program that tells you the ugly truth after the fact—Guess what? You ran out of money before the end of the month *again!*—is not much help."

With the strain of unemployment and the constant calls from various collection agencies and creditors, Rob was determined to find something better. While searching for something better, Rob was introduced to a computer-based envelope budgeting system. After reading about the philosophy surrounding this budgeting method, Rob decided to give it a try. "That first week, we used it every day," Rob said. "I was sold on it by the third day and knew I could never go back to our previous financial management system."

Rob found a new job, with only a minor cut in pay, and then set out to reorganize their finances. The Joseph family worked to live within their means by adopting and using the envelope budgeting principles. Within a few short months they managed to turn everything around. "Today we 'walked away' from Colleen's Mercedes SUV. The lease had ended and we decided against buying it out. We just dropped it off at the dealership and went across the street. We bought a used minivan with cash. No car payment!" Rob exclaims, "And it's a great car!"

Rob continues, "That's one example of two dozen major tactical changes we have made. The ironic thing is that instead of feeling deprived, we feel in control for the first time in many years. Shrinking credit card debt. No car payments. Just a monthly mortgage payment and a few utility and school checks to write each month. And the best part is that we now have a five-figure bank balance growing to go along with the six-figure salary. Finally!"

Rob and Colleen learned, as have many like them, that financial fitness is not a function of how much you earn but rather what you choose to do with the money that you do earn. The true secret lies in spending less than you earn on a consistent basis. Even though they had great intentions through the years, it was not until Rob and Colleen adopted the envelope method of budgeting that they were able to clearly see their way to living within their means. You are well on your way to following in their footsteps. ■

After tracking your transactions over the past few weeks, you should be able to identify spending habits that you can change. And the great part is that because you have made the commitment to live within your means, you will find it much easier to make the necessary adjustments. As you continue down this path, you'll find that your behavior and habits will begin to change and align with your new commitment.

During week 3, you will need to continue tracking each of your transactions, just as you have for the last two weeks. Check and date each of the following actions when you have completed them for the week.

■ ACTION 1—WEEK 3: Record All Deposits *(See Action 5, Week 1, page 46.)*

Record all deposits on your bank account registers and appropriately allocate them to your envelope spending accounts according to your monthly income allocation plan. Record the appropriate amount on each of your envelope spending account registers.

Check _________ Date ____________________

■ ACTION 2—WEEK 3: Track All Expenses *(See Action 5, Week 1, page 46.)*

Track all expense transactions for the week by recording them on the appropriate bank account register and envelope spending account registers.

Check ________ Date ____________________

■ ACTION 3—WEEK 3: Track All Credit Card Transactions *(See Action 5, Week 1, page 46.)*

Track all credit card transactions for the week by recording them on the appropriate credit card account register, envelope spending account registers, and credit card repayment register.

Check ________ Date ____________________

■ ACTION 4—WEEK 3: Check Your Balances *(See Action 6, Week 1, page 55.)*

Make appropriate spending decisions by spending from the balance remaining in each of your envelope spending accounts. Make any transfers between envelope spending accounts that are appropriate.

Check ________ Date ____________________

Way to go! You are now ready for week 4!

Track

Success Story

Dan came across the computer-based envelope budgeting system and realized immediately the possibilities that it would offer to his family's financial situation. He discovered after a few months of procrastination that he was nervous about giving up his old ways of using another system to manage his personal finances. Despite the fact that Dan felt his old system was not helping him and his family appropriately manage their spending, it was what he and Kathy, his wife, were familiar with. However, with Dan and Kathy both using their various accounts, they needed to adopt a method that would allow both of them to know exactly where their money was going every month and how much they had left.

They finally took the plunge and adopted the envelope method of budgeting. After only a short ten months, they have completely eliminated using the overdraft protection on their account, a practice that had occurred each and every month in the past. As Dan explains, "I think the biggest thing was that we just didn't know for sure where our money was going. It's hard to fix a problem when you don't even know what the problem is!"

Now that they have a way to track all the bills, payments, spending, and balances in real time, Dan and Kathy have not only cut out the overspending but are now able to save for future purchases and unexpected expenses as well. They have already set aside $1,000 toward this year's Christmas, which is still two months away. Their four young children are going to be thrilled Christmas morning, and, best of all, Dan and Kathy won't be going into debt to create that magic moment. They have a balance in their savings account, and they have also been saving for a family vacation next summer. Dan states: "Maybe the rest of the world has found a way to do this on their own, but we sure hadn't. It wasn't until we adopted the envelope budgeting method that we were able to achieve these things.

"Best of all is the peace of mind that we now enjoy," Dan continues. "Knowing that our financial house is in order and that we will be better off tomorrow than we are today gives us a sense of peace and security." ■

Dan and Kathy have found the financial path least traveled. With the help of an envelope budgeting system, they have been able to influence the direction of change in their financial life. Each day seems to be brighter than the last, leaving them with a feeling of great satisfaction and peace. These are just a few of the benefits that come from living based on the commitments you have made.

During week 4, you will need to continue tracking each of your transactions, just as you have been doing since beginning your envelope budgeting program. Check and date each of the following actions when you have completed them for the week.

■ ACTION 1—WEEK 4: Record All Deposits *(See Action 5, Week 1, page 46.)*

Record all deposits on your bank account registers and allocate them appropriately to each of your spending accounts according to your monthly income allocation plan. Record the appropriate amount on each of your envelope spending account registers.

Check ________ Date ____________________

■ ACTION 2—WEEK 4: Track All Expenses *(See Action 5, Week 1, page 46.)*

Track all expense transactions for the week by recording them on the appropriate bank account register and envelope spending account registers.

Check ________ Date ____________________

■ ACTION 3—WEEK 4: Track All Credit Card Transactions *(See Action 5, Week 1, page 46.)*

Track all credit card transactions for the week by recording them on the appropriate credit card account register, envelope spending account registers, and credit card repayment register.

Check ________ Date ____________________

■ ACTION 4—WEEK 4: Check Your Balances *(See Action 6, Week 1, page 55.)*

Make appropriate spending decisions by spending from the balance remaining in each of your envelope spending accounts. Make any transfers between envelope spending accounts that are appropriate.

Check __________ Date ______________________

Congratulations, you have now completed one-third of your 12-week financial fitness program. Let's move on to week 5!

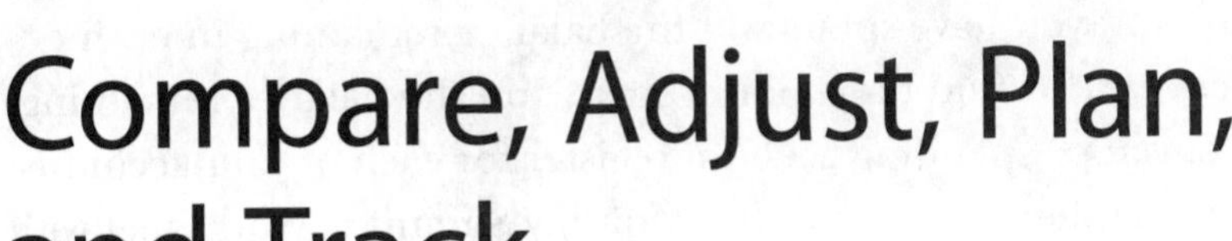

Compare, Adjust, Plan, and Track

Completing the first few weeks of the 12-week *Money for Life* Financial Fitness Program is the most difficult part. Not only have you prepared a plan, but you have also spent the last four weeks carefully tracking your progress. You have begun to adopt new thought processes, which are creating new behaviors and habits. These behaviors and habits are assisting you to reach your stated objectives. Congratulations for following the financial path least traveled! You have accomplished something few others have in our society.

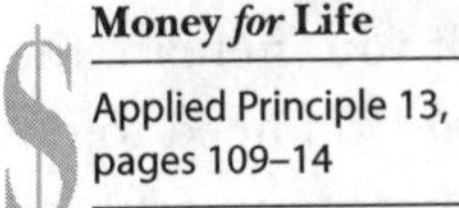

Money *for* Life

Applied Principle 13, pages 109–14

During the preceding four weeks, you successfully implemented comprehensive tracking and good decision making. With this process solidly in place, it is important to define a regular interval for the purpose of *comparing* your actual spending with your spending plan—the third phase of the Success Cycle.

For most people, the best interval for this comparison is monthly. You could do it more frequently, but less often than monthly may prove to be problematic. If you don't review your progress often enough, it is difficult to make the appropriate adjustments on a timely basis—equivalent to checking your compass every mile versus every 100 yards. Obviously, it's very easy to go significantly off your course if you only check each mile.

■ ACTION 1—WEEK 5: Compare and Make Adjustments

Perform a monthly comparison with the envelope system that you have chosen by completing the three steps described in the following sections.

STEP 1: Review Your Envelope Spending Account Balances

The first step is to review your envelope spending account balances. Determine how much is left in each envelope at the end of the month and how much was spent during the month. You need to make sure this calculation includes any money transferred from another envelope. If you are using the paper ledger system, you will need to complete the Monthly Envelope Spending Account Summary Worksheet found in Appendix B, Figure B.13. Complete the worksheet by determining the amount you have spent and the balance remaining in each envelope spending account. To find the amount spent and the balance remaining, simply refer to the envelope spending account register for each of your accounts. See Figure 5.1 for a completed sample of the Monthly Summary Worksheet with the recorded information on amount spent and balance remaining.

Mvelopes® Personal Tutorial: If you are using Mvelopes Personal, click on the Current Envelope Balance Summary report in the Reports section of the Main Toolbar. This will allow you to generate a monthly envelope spending account summary report.

Depending on the system you are using, with either your Mvelopes Personal Envelope Spending Account Summary Report or your Monthly Summary Worksheet in hand, compare the amount actually spent during the month with the amount that you had planned to spend. During this step, you will see envelope spending accounts for which you may need to increase your monthly allocation of income and those for which you may be able to reduce your allocation. Remember that when you make adjustments in income allocations, you need to make sure your spending plan is still balanced. For example, if you increase the monthly allocation for the clothing envelope spending account, you need to decrease the allocation to another envelope spending account or accounts by the same amount. The total amount of net monthly income must equal the total amount of envelope spending account allocations. Making these adjustments allows you to tighten your plan for the next month.

If you are using the paper ledger envelope system, record your desired adjustments on the Monthly Envelope Spending Account Summary Worksheet. See Figure 5.2 for an example of how these adjustments are made.

Mvelopes® Personal Tutorial: If you are using Mvelopes Personal, click on Spending Plan from the View tab on the main menu bar to make your adjustments.

You may often find that you didn't include a particular area of spending that needs to be tracked. In that case, you need to create a new envelope spending account. Again, remember that when you create a new envelope spending account, you need to reduce the allocation to other accounts by the amount you decide to allocate to the new account.

At times, you may also find you are no longer using a particular envelope spending account. An example of this may be an account set up to save for the purchase of a major item. After the purchase is complete, you no longer need to set aside money for that envelope spending account on a monthly basis. This

FIGURE 5.1 Sample Monthly Envelope Spending Account Summary

Monthly Envelope Spending Account Summary — Date: September

Envelope Spending Accounts	Monthly Spending Plan	Amount Spent	Remaining Balance	Spending Plan Adjustments	New Monthly Spending Plan
Monthly Required					
Mortgage	$1,422.00	$1,422.00	$0.00		
Home Equity Loan	142.00	142.00	0.00		
Auto Loan	517.00	517.00	0.00		
American Express	75.00	150.00	0.00		
Visa	95.00	95.00	95.00		
Student Loan	142.00	142.00	0.00		
Savings	300.00	0.00	300.00		
Department Store	75.00	75.00	0.00		
Music Lessons	60.00	55.00	65.00		
Fitness Club	30.00	30.00	0.00		
School Lunch	20.00	17.00	3.00		
Auto Insurance	140.00	140.00	140.00		
Cable	35.00	35.00	35.00		
Power	150.00	135.00	165.00		
Natural Gas	60.00	40.00	80.00		
House Security	23.00	23.00	23.00		
Water, Sewer & Garbage	50.00	50.00	50.00		
Day Care	500.00	500.00	500.00		
Monthly Discretionary					
Auto Fuel	$225.00	$245.00	$49.00		
Babysitter	30.00	15.00	35.00		
Clothing	175.00	165.00	60.00		
Entertainment	95.00	75.00	40.00		
Dining Out	75.00	90.00	15.00		
Groceries	400.00	370.00	230.00		
Haircuts	35.00	25.00	10.00		
Spending—Ryan	50.00	50.00	0.00		
Spending—Christine	50.00	50.00	0.00		
Personal Items	50.00	42.00	8.00		
Supplies	10.00	20.00	20.00		
Phone—Home	75.00	85.00	40.00		
Phone—Mobile	100.00	75.00	25.00		
Books & Magazines	10.00	0.00	10.00		
Periodic Required					
Auto Registration	$30.00	$0.00	$30.00		
Property Tax	165.00	0.00	165.00		
Homeowner's Insurance	75.00	0.00	75.00		
Life Insurance	50.00	0.00	50.00		
Periodic Discretionary					
Dental Deductible	$25.00	$5.00	$1.23		
Doctor Visits Deductible	60.00	0.00	0.00		
Birthday Gifts	35.00	45.00	–45.00		
Holiday Gifts	75.00	0.00	0.00		
Other Gifts	15.00	15.00	–15.00		
Auto Maintenance	115.00	35.00	–35.00		
House Maintenance	75.00	55.00	–55.00		
Vacation	175.00	0.00	0.00		
Donations	125.00	125.00	–125.00		
Total:	$6,236.00	$5,155.00	$2,044.23		

FIGURE 5.2 Adjustments to the Monthly Envelope Spending Account Summary

Monthly Envelope Spending Account Summary — Date: September

Envelope Spending Accounts	Monthly Spending Plan	Amount Spent	Remaining Balance	Spending Plan Adjustments	New Monthly Spending Plan
Monthly Required					
Mortgage	$1,422.00	$1,422.00	$0.00		
Home Equity Loan	142.00	142.00	0.00		
Auto Loan	517.00	517.00	0.00		
American Express	75.00	150.00	0.00		
Visa	95.00	95.00	95.00		
Student Loan	142.00	142.00	0.00		
Savings	300.00	0.00	300.00		
Department Store	75.00	75.00	0.00		
Music Lessons	60.00	55.00	65.00		
Fitness Club	30.00	30.00	0.00		
School Lunch	20.00	17.00	3.00		
Auto Insurance	140.00	140.00	140.00		
Cable	35.00	35.00	35.00		
Power	150.00	135.00	165.00	–$10.00	
Natural Gas	60.00	40.00	80.00	–10.00	
House Security	23.00	23.00	23.00		
Water, Sewer & Garbage	50.00	50.00	50.00		
Day Care	500.00	500.00	500.00		
Monthly Discretionary					
Auto Fuel	$225.00	$245.00	$49.00	+$20.00	
Babysitter	30.00	15.00	35.00		
Clothing	175.00	165.00	60.00		
Entertainment	95.00	75.00	40.00		
Dining Out	75.00	90.00	15.00	–15.00	
Groceries	400.00	370.00	230.00		
Haircuts	35.00	25.00	10.00		
Spending—Ryan	50.00	50.00	0.00		
Spending—Christine	50.00	50.00	0.00		
Personal Items	50.00	42.00	8.00		
Supplies	10.00	20.00	20.00	+10.00	
Phone—Home	75.00	85.00	40.00	+5.00	
Phone—Mobile	100.00	75.00	25.00		
Books & Magazines	10.00	0.00	10.00		
Periodic Required					
Auto Registration	$30.00	$0.00	$30.00		
Property Tax	165.00	0.00	165.00		
Homeowner's Insurance	75.00	0.00	75.00		
Life Insurance	50.00	0.00	50.00		
Periodic Discretionary					
Dental Deductible	$25.00	$5.00	$1.23		
Doctor Visits Deductible	60.00	60.00	0.00		
Birthday Gifts	35.00	45.00	–45.00		
Holiday Gifts	75.00	0.00	0.00		
Other Gifts	15.00	15.00	–15.00		
Auto Maintenance	115.00	35.00	–35.00		
House Maintenance	75.00	55.00	–55.00		
Vacation	175.00	0.00	0.00		
Donations	125.00	125.00	–125.00		
Total:	$6,236.00	$5,155.00	$2,044.23	$0.00	

allows you to reallocate the income that has been going to that envelope spending account to another account or accounts.

If you are using the paper ledger system, you need to make these adjustments on the Monthly Envelope Spending Account Summary Worksheet. See Figure 5.3 for an example of adding an envelope spending account and making the associated adjustments.

Mvelopes® Personal Tutorial: If you are using Mvelopes Personal, click on Spending Plan from the View tab on the main menu bar to make your adjustments.

Once you have finished making all adjustments, complete the Monthly Envelope Spending Account Summary Worksheet amounts by recording your new monthly spending plan in the final column. Refer to Figure 5.4 for an example of a new monthly spending plan.

Mvelopes® Personal Tutorial: If you are using Mvelopes Personal, your spending plan will be automatically updated as you make adjustments.

STEP 2: Transfer Your Savings and Set New Beginning Balances

Once you have completed the review of your envelope spending account balances and made appropriate income allocation adjustments, you are ready to move on to the next step. Each month, you need to set the beginning balances for each envelope spending account. The analysis for this process differs, depending on the type of envelope spending account.

Monthly required envelope spending accounts. Let's first take a look at your monthly required envelope spending accounts. Because the spending associated with these accounts is usually a fixed amount with spending taking place each month, your ending account balance should be zero, meaning you have spent the total amount of money set aside in that account by the end of the month. Remember, these envelope spending accounts include things like required debt payments, some utility payments, monthly insurance payments, and so on. Unless your payment amount has changed, in which case you would need to make an adjustment in the amount of monthly allocation to that account, your beginning balance for these accounts will be zero.

Monthly discretionary envelope spending accounts. Next, let's look at monthly discretionary envelope spending accounts. If, at the end of the month, you have a remaining balance in these accounts, you have two choices: Roll the balance over to the next month, in which case the ending balance will become the beginning balance, or transfer the remaining balance to another account and set the beginning balance to zero.

FIGURE 5.3 Sample Monthly Envelope Spending Account Summary Report with Adjustments

Monthly Envelope Spending Account Summary — Date: September

Envelope Spending Accounts	Monthly Spending Plan	Amount Spent	Remaining Balance	Spending Plan Adjustments	New Monthly Spending Plan
Monthly Required					
Mortgage	$1,422.00	$1,422.00	$0.00		
Home Equity Loan	142.00	142.00	0.00		
Auto Loan	517.00	517.00	0.00		
American Express	75.00	150.00	0.00		
Visa	95.00	95.00	95.00		
Student Loan	142.00	142.00	0.00		
Savings	300.00	0.00	300.00		
Department Store	75.00	75.00	0.00		
Music Lessons	60.00	55.00	65.00		
Fitness Club	30.00	30.00	0.00		
School Lunch	20.00	17.00	3.00		
Auto Insurance	140.00	140.00	140.00		
Cable	35.00	35.00	35.00		
Power	150.00	135.00	165.00	–$10.00	
Natural Gas	60.00	40.00	80.00	–10.00	
House Security	23.00	23.00	23.00		
Water, Sewer & Garbage	50.00	50.00	50.00		
Day Care	500.00	500.00	500.00		
Monthly Discretionary					
Auto Fuel	$225.00	$245.00	$49.00	$20.00	
Babysitter	30.00	15.00	35.00		
Clothing	175.00	165.00	60.00		
Entertainment	95.00	75.00	40.00	–20.00	
Dining Out	75.00	90.00	15.00	–15.00	
Groceries	400.00	370.00	230.00	–25.00	
Haircuts	35.00	25.00	10.00		
Spending—Ryan	50.00	50.00	0.00		
Spending—Christine	50.00	50.00	0.00		
Personal Items	50.00	42.00	8.00		
Supplies	10.00	20.00	20.00	$10.00	
Phone—Home	75.00	85.00	40.00	5.00	
Phone—Mobile	100.00	75.00	25.00		
Books & Magazines	10.00	0.00	10.00		
Dry Cleaning				45.00	
Periodic Required					
Auto Registration	$30.00	$0.00	$30.00		
Property Tax	165.00	0.00	165.00		
Homeowner's Insurance	75.00	0.00	75.00		
Life Insurance	50.00	0.00	50.00		
Periodic Discretionary					
Dental Deductible	$25.00	$5.00	$1.23		
Doctor Visits Deductible	60.00	0.00	0.00		
Birthday Gifts	35.00	45.00	–45.00		
Holiday Gifts	75.00	0.00	0.00		
Other Gifts	15.00	15.00	–15.00		
Auto Maintenance	115.00	35.00	–35.00		
House Maintenance	75.00	55.00	–55.00		
Vacation	175.00	0.00	0.00		
Donations	125.00	125.00	–125.00		
Total:	$6,236.00	$5,155.00	$2,044.23	$0.00	

FIGURE 5.4 Completed Monthly Envelope Spending Account Summary Worksheet

Monthly Envelope Spending Account Summary — Date: *September*

Envelope Spending Accounts	Monthly Spending Plan	Amount Spent	Remaining Balance	Spending Plan Adjustments	New Monthly Spending Plan
Monthly Required					
Mortgage	$1,422.00	$1,422.00	$0.00		$1,422.00
Home Equity Loan	142.00	142.00	0.00		142.00
Auto Loan	517.00	517.00	0.00		517.00
American Express	75.00	150.00	0.00		75.00
Visa	95.00	95.00	95.00		95.00
Student Loan	142.00	142.00	0.00		142.00
Savings	300.00	0.00	300.00		300.00
Department Store	75.00	75.00	0.00		75.00
Music Lessons	60.00	55.00	65.00		60.00
Fitness Club	30.00	30.00	0.00		30.00
School Lunch	20.00	17.00	3.00		20.00
Auto Insurance	140.00	140.00	140.00		140.00
Cable	35.00	35.00	35.00		35.00
Power	150.00	135.00	165.00	−$10.00	140.00
Natural Gas	60.00	40.00	80.00	−10.00	50.00
House Security	23.00	23.00	23.00		23.00
Water, Sewer & Garbage	50.00	50.00	50.00		50.00
Day Care	500.00	500.00	500.00		500.00
Monthly Discretionary					
Auto Fuel	$225.00	$245.00	$49.00	+$20.00	$245.00
Babysitter	30.00	15.00	35.00		30.00
Clothing	175.00	165.00	60.00		175.00
Entertainment	95.00	75.00	40.00	−20.00	75.00
Dining Out	75.00	90.00	15.00	−15.00	60.00
Groceries	400.00	370.00	230.00	−25.00	375.00
Haircuts	35.00	25.00	10.00		35.00
Spending—Ryan	50.00	50.00	0.00		50.00
Spending—Christine	50.00	50.00	0.00		50.00
Personal Items	50.00	42.00	8.00		50.00
Supplies	10.00	20.00	20.00	+10.00	20.00
Phone—Home	75.00	85.00	40.00	+5.00	80.00
Phone—Mobile	100.00	75.00	25.00		100.00
Books & Magazines	10.00	0.00	10.00		10.00
Dry Cleaning				+45.00	45.00
Periodic Required					
Auto Registration	$30.00	$0.00	$30.00		$30.00
Property Tax	165.00	0.00	165.00		165.00
Homeowner's Insurance	75.00	0.00	75.00		75.00
Life Insurance	50.00	0.00	50.00		50.00
Periodic Discretionary					
Dental Deductible	$25.00	$5.00	$1.23		$25.00
Doctor Visits Deductible	60.00	0.00	0.00		60.00
Birthday Gifts	35.00	45.00	−45.00		35.00
Holiday Gifts	75.00	0.00	0.00		75.00
Other Gifts	15.00	15.00	−15.00		15.00
Auto Maintenance	115.00	35.00	−35.00		115.00
House Maintenance	75.00	55.00	−55.00		75.00
Vacation	175.00	0.00	0.00		175.00
Donations	125.00	125.00	−125.00		125.00
Total:	$6,236.00	$5,155.00	$2,044.23	$0.00	$6,236.00

These envelope spending accounts represent an opportunity to move additional money to savings, debt repayment, or investments. For example, if you normally set aside $500 for groceries each month, and you have a balance remaining in your groceries account of $45 at the end of the month, you can transfer that amount to savings, investments, or additional debt repayment. You should feel comfortable with this transfer, because next month you will allocate another $500 to your groceries account. This amount should be enough to cover your expenses for the next month. As a result, the $45 should be viewed as real savings. As you can see, by transferring the remaining balance in each of your monthly discretionary accounts and setting the beginning balance to zero, you can significantly increase the amount you are saving, investing, or adding to debt reduction.

Periodic required envelope spending accounts. Let's next look at your periodic required accounts. The idea behind these accounts is to set aside money on a monthly basis for future required expenses that you will pay quarterly, annually, and so on. These accounts include things like annual property tax payments, periodic insurance payments, annual auto registration fees, and the like. Because you need the balance for these accounts to grow from month to month, you should roll the ending balance over, and it should become your beginning balance for the next month. As is the case with the monthly required accounts, if the amount of the expense changes, you need to make an adjustment in the amount of income you allocate to this account each month. Remember, this requires an offsetting adjustment to another account or accounts to ensure your spending plan remains balanced.

Periodic discretionary envelope spending accounts. Finally, let's take a look at the periodic discretionary envelope spending accounts. These accounts include things like vacations, holiday spending, gifts, house maintenance, and so on. The objective for these accounts is also to set aside money for future spending requirements. However, because these accounts represent discretionary spending, you should constantly monitor the balances to determine if they are sufficient to address your spending needs. If you believe your spending requirements for one of these envelope spending accounts will increase in the future, you need to determine how much more of your monthly income you should be allocating to that area. The same is true if you believe your spending requirements may be less than originally anticipated.

One of the ways to treat these accounts is to determine an annual requirement and continue setting money aside until the balance in the account has reached that amount. Once it has, you may choose to transfer any amount over that annual requirement to savings, investments, or debt repayment. An example of this would be your house maintenance account. Let's say that you believe you will need to spend $1,200 on house repairs and general maintenance over the next 12 months. Based on this number, you will be allocating $100 each month to the house maintenance account. Basically, you are saying that you want to have

$1,200 set aside for any repairs that may be necessary. If after 13 months, the balance in this account exceeds your $1,200 annual repair estimate because you have had little or no repair expenses, you can transfer the amount above this number to another account. Once you have reached the $1,200 limit, you are able to transfer the $100 monthly allocation currently assigned to house maintenance to another account, such as savings, investments, or debt repayment, in each subsequent month. However, you will always have the $1,200 set aside if it is required. After several months of lower-than-expected repairs, you may determine that the annual spending estimate is too high, and you can make an adjustment to the monthly allocation in your spending plan.

After you have completed a review of each of your envelope spending accounts, make the appropriate envelope spending account transfers to set the beginning balances for next month. You should already know how to make envelope spending account to envelope spending account transfers. If you need to review this process, see Action 6, Week 1, page 55.

STEP 3: Reconcile Your Envelope Spending Accounts and Bank Accounts

In order to maintain accurate information, you need to reconcile your accounts at the end of each month. First reconcile your bank accounts based on your normal procedure. Remember that the combined total of your bank account balances should equal the combined total of all of your envelope spending accounts. In other words, if you have $3,000 in your bank account, the combined balance of your envelope spending accounts should equal $3,000. If adjustments are made in your bank account as a result of your reconciliation, you need to make a corresponding adjustment to one or more of your envelope spending accounts. If you are using the paper ledger system, be sure to include these adjustments on your bank account register and your envelope spending account registers.

Also, if the combined balance of your envelope spending accounts does not match your bank account balance, you then need to make an appropriate adjustment to one or more of your envelope spending accounts. Again, make sure you record these adjustments on your account registers.

This monthly reconciliation process ensures that you can depend on the balance information in each of your envelope spending accounts. This is very important when you are making purchase decisions based on this information.

Complete a monthly reconciliation for each of your bank accounts.

Mvelopes® Personal Tutorial: If you are using Mvelopes Personal, click the Tutorial icon on the main toolbar and select the Bank Account Reconciliation tutorial under Other Tutorials to learn how to do bank account reconciliation.

Once you have completed the reconciliation process and have recorded any adjustment to the appropriate bank and envelope spending account registers, make sure that the combined total of your bank accounts is equal to the combined total of your envelope spending accounts. If you are using Mvelopes Personal, this calculation is done automatically and the system is always in balance.

■ ACTION 2—WEEK 5: Update the Monthly Allocation History

You have just completed one trip around the Success Cycle. You created your spending plan, meticulously tracked your spending, compared your actual spending to the plan, and made appropriate adjustments based on these comparisons. Now that you understand this process, it is important that you repeat it every month. Each time you compare and make adjustments, your plan becomes more accurate. Every time you track expenses and make spending decisions based on the balances that remain, you find other ways to save money. You'll be surprised how easy using the envelope system and following the Success Cycle can be. During your 12-week financial fitness program, you complete the Success Cycle three times. By the time you have made monthly adjustments for the third time, you will have a very accurate spending plan.

One of the great benefits of the monthly review is the opportunity to sit together with your partner and review your progress toward achieving financial objectives and to recommit yourselves to reaching these objectives together. Utilizing the envelope system and following the Success Cycle can bring significant harmony into your life. Being on the same financial page and working together to meet your financial objectives can be one of the most rewarding pursuits you can have as a couple.

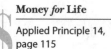

Money *for* Life
Applied Principle 14, page 115

You may recall that the words *Financial Fitness* are on the inside of the Success Cycle chart. As you continue to follow the Success Cycle on a monthly basis, you will become increasingly more financially fit. Financial fitness is a process, not a single event in time. By moving down this path, you are well on your way to achieving your objective!

You are now prepared to begin your next trip around the Success Cycle. If you are using Mvelopes Personal, all of the adjustments that you have just made have been recorded and your new monthly spending plan has been set. If you are using the paper ledger system, you will need to complete the Monthly Allocation History Worksheet in Appendix B, Figure B.14.

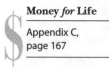

Money *for* Life
Appendix C, page 167

To complete this form you will first need to record the history for the first month. List each of the envelope spending accounts in the first column and record the allocation amounts from your first month's spending plan. In the next column, record the total amount of income that you allocated to each envelope spending account, including any allocations from savings if your income is primarily variable in nature.

Once you have completed this column, record the amount each envelope spending account was underfunded during the month. This is determined by subtracting the actual allocation amount from the planned allocation amount for each envelope spending account. Refer to your envelope spending account registers to see the amount you actually allocated. Record this amount in the appropriate column.

Next, record your new monthly spending plan in the next column. This is the amount taken from the last column of the Monthly Envelope Spending Account Summary Worksheet you completed earlier. (See Figure 5.4, on page 71.)

Finally, calculate the amount of next month's required allocations by adding the total amount underfunded this month to the new monthly spending plan amounts. In our example, a number of the periodic discretionary accounts were not funded during the last month, so that amount must be carried forward and added to the next month's required allocations. See Figure 5.5 for an example of a completed Monthly Allocation History Worksheet.

Once you have completed this step, prepare the monthly income allocation plan for month 2. To do this, record each of your envelope spending accounts in the appropriate sections of column one. Next, record your new monthly required allocation amounts for each of your envelope spending accounts. These amounts are your new monthly required allocation from the last column of the Monthly Allocation History Worksheet.

Next, record each income you will receive during the month and determine how it will be allocated. See Figure 5.6 for an example of how to complete the Monthly Income Allocation Plan Worksheet for month 2.

Completing both the monthly allocation history and the monthly income allocation plan allows you to keep track of your funding requirements as your income varies from month to month. For example, if you receive a paycheck every two weeks, you receive two paychecks for ten months of the year and three paychecks for two months of the year. On your allocation plan, you may decide to put off funding some of your periodic discretionary envelope spending accounts like vacations or holiday spending until you receive a third check in a month. Completing the monthly allocation history and income allocation plan allows you to keep track of which accounts have been funded appropriately and which still require additional allocations. It also allows you to successfully track your allocations if your income is variable in nature. If you are using Mvelopes Personal, these calculations are handled automatically as you prepare your funding plan and assign the income you receive to an income profile.

■ ACTION 3—WEEK 5: Create a Debt Elimination Plan

Money *for* Life
Principle 15, pages 116–19

One of the most crippling effects on personal financial fitness is debt. Debt is every bit as damaging to your financial health as extra weight is to your physical health. Losing your debt load can be the most financially liberating thing you will ever do. Continuing to add to your debt will likely be the most financially restricting thing you can do.

FIGURE 5.5 Completed Monthly Allocation History Worksheet

Monthly Allocation History — Month: September

Envelope Spending Accounts	Total Monthly Required Allocation	Total Monthly Actual Allocation	Total Monthly Amount Underfunded	New Monthly Spending Plan	New Monthly Required Allocation
Monthly Required					
Mortgage	$1,422.00	$1,422.00		$1,422.00	$1,422.00
Home Equity Loan	142.00	142.00		142.00	142.00
Auto Loan	517.00	517.00		517.00	517.00
American Express	75.00	75.00		75.00	75.00
Visa	95.00	95.00		95.00	95.00
Student Loan	142.00	142.00		142.00	142.00
Savings	300.00	300.00		300.00	300.00
Department Store	75.00	75.00		75.00	75.00
Music Lessons	60.00	60.00		60.00	60.00
Fitness Club	30.00	30.00		30.00	30.00
School Lunch	20.00	20.00		20.00	20.00
Auto Insurance	140.00	140.00		140.00	140.00
Cable	35.00	35.00		35.00	35.00
Power	150.00	150.00		140.00	140.00
Natural Gas	60.00	60.00		50.00	50.00
House Security	23.00	23.00		23.00	23.00
Water, Sewer, & Garbage	50.00	50.00		50.00	50.00
Day Care	500.00	500.00		500.00	500.00
Monthly Discretionary					
Auto Fuel	$225.00	$225.00		$245.00	$245.00
Babysitter	30.00	30.00		30.00	30.00
Clothing	175.00	175.00		175.00	175.00
Entertainment	95.00	95.00		75.00	75.00
Dining Out	75.00	75.00		60.00	60.00
Groceries	400.00	400.00		375.00	375.00
Haircuts	35.00	35.00		35.00	35.00
Spending—Ryan	50.00	50.00		50.00	50.00
Spending—Christine	50.00	50.00		50.00	50.00
Personal Items	50.00	50.00		50.00	50.00
Supplies	10.00	10.00		20.00	20.00
Phone—Home	75.00	75.00		80.00	80.00
Phone—Mobile	100.00	100.00		100.00	100.00
Books & Magazines	10.00	10.00		10.00	10.00
Dry Cleaning				45.00	45.00
Periodic Required					
Auto Registration	$30.00	$30.00		$30.00	$30.00
Property Tax	165.00	165.00		165.00	165.00
Homeowner's Insurance	75.00	75.00		75.00	75.00
Life Insurance	50.00	50.00		50.00	50.00
Periodic Discretionary					
Dental Deductible	$25.00	$6.23	$18.77	$25.00	$43.77
Doctor Visits Deductible	60.00		60.00	60.00	120.00
Birthday Gifts	35.00		35.00	35.00	70.00
Holiday Gifts	75.00		75.00	75.00	150.00
Other Gifts	15.00		15.00	15.00	30.00
Auto Maintenance	115.00		115.00	115.00	230.00
House Maintenance	75.00		75.00	75.00	150.00
Vacation	175.00		175.00	175.00	350.00
Donations	125.00		125.00	125.00	250.00
Total:	$6,236.00	$5,542.23	$693.77	$6,236.00	$6,929.77

FIGURE 5.6 Monthly Income Allocation Plan for Month 2

Monthly Income Allocation Plan				Month:	*October*		
	Income Source	Medical One	Wash. Elem.	Medical One	Wash. Elem.	Medical One Bonus	Medical One
	Date of Receipt	10-03	10-15	10-17	10-31	10-01	Check 25 & 26
	Amount of Income	$1,772.78	$1,048.34	$1,772.78	$1,048.33	$1,055.00	Yet to Be Received
Envelope Spending Accounts	**Monthly Required Allocation**	**Allocation Amount**	**Allocation Amount**	**Allocation Amount**	**Allocation Amount**	**Allocation Amount**	**Allocation Amount**
Monthly Required							
Mortgage	$1,422.00	$1,422.00					
Home Equity Loan	142.00	142.00					
Auto Loan	517.00	208.78	$308.22				
American Express	75.00		75.00				
Visa	95.00		95.00				
Student Loan	142.00		142.00				
Savings	300.00		300.00				
Department Store	75.00		75.00				
Music Lessons	60.00		53.12	$6.88			
Fitness Club	30.00			30.00			
School Lunch	20.00			20.00			
Auto Insurance	140.00			140.00			
Cable	35.00			35.00			
Power	140.00			140.00			
Natural Gas	50.00			50.00			
House Security	23.00			23.00			
Water, Sewer & Garbage	50.00			50.00			
Day Care	500.00			500.00			
Monthly Discretionary							
Auto Fuel	$245.00			$245.00			
Babysitter	30.00			30.00			
Clothing	175.00			175.00			
Entertainment	75.00			75.00			
Dining Out	60.00			60.00			
Groceries	375.00			192.92	$182.10		
Haircuts	35.00				35.00		
Spending—Ryan	50.00				50.00		
Spending—Christine	50.00				50.00		
Personal Items	50.00				50.00		
Supplies	20.00				20.00		
Phone—Home	80.00				80.00		
Phone—Mobile	100.00				100.00		
Books & Magazines	10.00				10.00		
Dry Cleaning	45.00				45.00		
Periodic Required							
Auto Registration	$30.00				$30.00		
Property Tax	165.00				165.00		
Homeowner's Insurance	75.00				75.00		
Life Insurance	50.00				50.00		
Periodic Discretionary							
Dental Deductible	$43.77				$43.77		
Doctor Visits Deductible	120.00				62.46	$57.54	
Birthday Gifts	70.00					70.00	
Holiday Gifts	150.00					150.00	
Other Gifts	30.00					30.00	
Auto Maintenance	230.00					230.00	
House Maintenance	150.00					150.00	
Vacation	350.00					350.00	
Donations	250.00					17.46	
Total Allocation:	$6,929.77	$1,772.78	$1,048.34	$1,772.78	$1,048.33	$1,055.00	

To successfully tackle personal debt, the first thing you must do is stop creating more. There is no way to begin reducing debt and eventually eliminate it if you are constantly increasing it by spending more than you make. Incorporating the principles necessary to live within your means is the first step to conquering personal debt. After you have been through the Success Cycle during the first month, you are prepared to begin an accelerated debt reduction program.

This debt reduction program is based on the debt roll-down principle, used to rapidly eliminate debt. Using an envelope system is the key ingredient to finding success with this approach. The debt roll-down principle works by determining the total monthly payment you can make toward debt repayment. Each time you pay off a debt, you add the payment for that debt to the monthly payment for the next priority debt, which accelerates the rate at which that second debt is paid. When the second debt is paid, you add the payment you have been making on this debt to the monthly payment for the third priority debt. This process is continued until all debt has been eliminated. The key is to continue making the same aggregate debt payment each month. Following this debt elimination principle can often assist you in eliminating all of your debt, including your mortgage, in as few as seven to eight years.

There are two ways to prioritize debt repayment: smallest outstanding balance to largest outstanding balance or highest interest rate to lowest interest rate. In most cases, you will eliminate your debt faster if you begin with the debt carrying the highest interest rate. However, if you prioritize smallest outstanding balance to largest outstanding balance, you may eliminate the first debt more quickly, thus providing motivation to continue with your debt reduction plan. You can quickly set up your rapid repayment plan by incorporating the following steps.

STEP 1: Create a List of All Debt

The first step is to create a list of all of your debts. This list should include the name of the debt or the creditor, the current outstanding balance, the minimum monthly payment, and the interest rate for each. The list should also be prioritized based on either interest rate (highest to lowest) or outstanding balance (smallest to largest). See Figure 5.7 for a sample listing of debt obligations, and then complete the Debt Summary Worksheet in Figure 5.8.

STEP 2: Check Your Monthly Envelope Spending Account Allocations

When you set up your monthly spending plan, you should have created an envelope spending account for each debt on your list. If you have left one out, you need to create an envelope spending account for this debt. If you need to create a new account, remember to make appropriate adjustments in your spending plan to maintain a balanced plan.

FIGURE 5.7 Sample Debt Obligation Summary

Debt Summary			
Debt Description	Balance	Payment	Interest Rate
Department Store	$287.00	$75.00	21.00%
Visa	2,500.00	95.00	18.50
American Express	3,000.00	75.00	14.50
Auto Loan	14,750.00	517.00	7.00
Mortgage	206,320.00	1,422.00	7.00

FIGURE 5.8 Debt Summary Worksheet

Debt Summary			Date: ________
Debt Description	Balance	Payment	Interest Rate

Each month, you will make your debt payments from the envelope spending accounts that you have created. After you pay off the first debt, you need to make an adjustment by adding the monthly allocation for that debt to the monthly allocation of the envelope spending account for the next priority debt. For example, let's say your first priority debt is a department store credit card. The amount of your monthly payment for this debt is $75, so the amount of income you allocate each month to the department store envelope spending account for that debt is $75. Your next highest priority debt is a Visa credit card. For this debt, your monthly payment is $95, so the amount of income you allocate to the Visa credit card envelope spending account each month is $95. After four months, you have paid off the department store debt. When you complete your monthly adjustment, you transfer any remaining balance from the department store envelope spending account to the Visa credit card envelope spending account. You will also adjust the monthly income allocation for the Visa credit card envelope spending account by adding the $75 to the $95. You now are making a monthly payment of $170 on the Visa credit card. This is repeated each time a debt is paid off. Before long, you will have eliminated all of your consumer debt and will be making much larger mortgage payments. See Figure 5.9 for an example of how the debt roll-down principle works.

STEP 3: Accelerate Your Debt Payment with Monthly Envelope Spending Account Transfers

Once you have created your debt elimination plan, you can begin to accelerate your debt repayment by transferring unused funds from your envelope spending accounts to your debt repayment accounts. You may recall the earlier example of transferring the balance remaining in monthly discretionary envelope spending accounts to savings, investments, or debt payments. Many people have found they can save an additional 10 percent each month by using an envelope system. If you have a net monthly income of $5,000, the additional amount you can save using the envelope system could be as much as $500. Imagine how quickly you can eliminate your consumer debt if you are adding 10 percent of your net monthly income to your debt payments each month.

For most people in our society, a significant portion of their monthly net income is dedicated to paying interest. Imagine how much money you can save and invest if you aren't paying interest. For most, this would represent several thousand dollars each year. Invested properly, this additional money may make a significant difference in your lifestyle later in life. Using an envelope system to successfully implement the debt roll-down principle helps you accomplish this objective.

To calculate how quickly you will be debt free using the debt roll-down principle with an accelerator, visit http://www.mvelopes.com/debt_calculator and enter the information from your Debt Summary Worksheet. The debt calculator determines the length of time it will take to be completely debt free. Print the debt elimination report and include it with your materials.

Use the Debt Payment Summary Worksheet found in Appendix B, Figure B.16, to track your rapid debt elimination progress.

FIGURE 5.9 Debt Roll-Down Example						
Debt Payment Summary						
Debt Priority Order	Debt: 1	Debt: 2	Debt: 3	Debt: 4	Debt: 5	Debt:
Description of Debt	Department Store	Visa Account	American Express	Auto Loan	Mortgage	
Month 1	$75.00	$95.00	$75.00	$517.00	$1,422.00	
Month 2	75.00	95.00	75.00	517.00	1,422.00	
Month 3	75.00	95.00	75.00	517.00	1,422.00	
Month 4	75.00	95.00	75.00	517.00	1,422.00	
Month 5	→	170.00	75.00	517.00	1,422.00	
Month 6		170.00	75.00	517.00	1,422.00	
Month 7		170.00	75.00	517.00	1,422.00	
Month 8		170.00	75.00	517.00	1,422.00	
Month 9		170.00	75.00	517.00	1,422.00	
Month 10		170.00	75.00	517.00	1,422.00	
Month 11		170.00	75.00	517.00	1,422.00	
Month 12		170.00	75.00	517.00	1,422.00	
Month 13		170.00	75.00	517.00	1,422.00	
Month 14		170.00	75.00	517.00	1,422.00	
Month 15		170.00	75.00	517.00	1,422.00	
Month 16		170.00	75.00	517.00	1,422.00	
Month 17		170.00	75.00	517.00	1,422.00	
Month 18		170.00	75.00	517.00	1,422.00	
Month 19		170.00	75.00	517.00	1,422.00	
Month 20		→	245.00	517.00	1,422.00	
Month 21			245.00	517.00	1,422.00	
Month 22			245.00	517.00	1,422.00	
Month 23			245.00	517.00	1,422.00	
Month 24			245.00	517.00	1,422.00	
Month 25			245.00	517.00	1,422.00	
Month 26			245.00	517.00	1,422.00	
Month 27			245.00	517.00	1,422.00	
Month 28			245.00	517.00	1,422.00	
Month 29			245.00	517.00	1,422.00	
Month 30			→	762.00	1,422.00	
Month 31				762.00	1,422.00	
Month 32				→	2,184.00	
Month						

During week 5, you will need to continue to track each of your transactions, just as you have been since beginning your envelope budgeting program. Check and date each of the following actions when you have completed them for the week.

■ ACTION 4—WEEK 5: Record All Deposits *(See Action 5, Week 1, page 46.)*

Record all deposits on your bank account registers and appropriately allocate them to each of your envelope spending accounts according to your monthly income allocation plan. Record the appropriate amount on each of your envelope spending account registers.

Check ________ Date ____________________

■ ACTION 5—WEEK 5: Track All Expenses *(See Action 5, Week 1, page 46.)*

Track all expense transactions for the week by recording them on the appropriate bank account register and envelope spending account registers.

Check ________ Date ____________________

■ ACTION 6—WEEK 5: Track All Credit Card Transactions *(See Action 5, Week 1, page 46.)*

Track all credit card transactions for the week by recording them on the appropriate credit card account register, envelope spending account registers, and credit card repayment register.

Check ________ Date ____________________

■ ACTION 7—WEEK 5: Check Your Balances *(See Action 6, Week 1, page 55.)*

Make appropriate and informed spending decisions by spending from the balance remaining in each of your envelope spending accounts. Make any transfers between envelope spending accounts that are appropriate.

Check ________ Date ____________________

You have now completed week 5! With your adjusted spending plan complete and a new debt elimination plan in place, you are ready to move on to week 6.

Track

Success Story

Joseph and Mary Agloro, a retired couple, travel several months out of each year. They load up their RV and drive off to find whatever adventures come their way. Depending on their mood, this could mean dancing the night away to jazz in New Orleans, crabbing off the docks at the Embarcadero in Newport, Oregon, or even taking in the majestic mountain scenery in Whistler, British Columbia.

Being on the road for three to four months at a time, Joseph and Mary, of course, found it difficult to manage their finances. Often in the past, deposits weren't recorded or purchases tracked. Not to mention the challenge of not getting mail! With payments being mailed from all corners of North America, late fees were often incurred and numerous bills were lost. Much of this would be piled up and waiting for them when they arrived home in Washington after a few fun-filled months away.

Luckily, Joseph and Mary were introduced to envelope budgeting principles and adopted the computer-based method! Now they can manage all their finances, bills, payments, and spending by simply logging on and downloading all of their transactions. They can take care of everything—from paying their credit card to the utility bills for their house back in Washington. It's fast, it's easy, and there's no more worry about lost bills, missed payments, and late fees! As Mary puts it, "Now, when traveling, we simply download our transactions every few days and immediately assign them to the proper envelope accounts. We can see everything quickly and easily right within our envelope system. No more having to go to all the different Web sites; and this way we can make the most of our precious few online minutes." She continues, "The envelope system has made a big difference for us and helped us relax and enjoy our life much more." ■

Many retired couples are finding the management of their finances on a limited fixed income very stressful and frustrating. With the help of the envelope budgeting system, Joseph and Mary Agloro were able to make positive changes in their financial life that have significantly reduced the level of stress and frustration they were experiencing. If they continue to apply the principles of envelope budgeting and proactively track and manage their spending, they will be able to more fully enjoy their retirement and do so within the limitation of their fixed budget.

To continue moving forward in a positive way during week 6, you will need to track each of your transactions, just as you have been since beginning your envelope budgeting program. Check and date each of the following actions when you have completed them for the week.

■ ACTION 1—WEEK 6: Record All Deposits *(See Action 5, Week 1, page 46.)*

Record all deposits on your bank account registers and appropriately allocate them to each of your envelope spending accounts according to your monthly income allocation plan. Record the appropriate amount on each of your envelope spending account registers.

Check ________ Date ____________________

■ ACTION 2—WEEK 6: Track All Expenses *(See Action 5, Week 1, page 46.)*

Track all expense transactions for the week by recording them on the appropriate bank account register and envelope spending account registers.

Check ________ Date ____________________

■ ACTION 3—WEEK 6: Track All Credit Card Transactions *(See Action 5, Week 1, page 46.)*

Track all credit card transactions for the week by recording them on the appropriate credit card account register, envelope spending account registers, and credit card repayment register.

Check ________ Date ____________________

■ ACTION 4—WEEK 6: Check Your Balances *(See Action 6, Week 1, page 55.)*

Make appropriate spending decisions by spending from the balance remaining in each of your envelope spending accounts. Make any transfers between envelope spending accounts that are appropriate.

Check __________ Date ______________________

Congratulations; you are now half finished with your 12-week financial fitness program. Tracking your transactions should be much easier now, and many new positive behaviors and habits should be taking hold. All of this should also be making a big difference in the way you interact with your personal finances on a daily basis. It's time now to move on to week 7.

Track

Success Story

Before Terri Hamilton found the envelope method of budgeting, she tried numerous other budgeting systems and was becoming more and more frustrated. They took too much time and were often hard to use and understand. These other systems just never seemed to function in a realistic manner, and Terri had trouble customizing them to the way she and her family spent. These systems didn't help her, in particular, with unusual or periodic expenses. Even when she knew they were coming up, she wasn't quite sure how to plan ahead for them.

Terri's spending and the spending of her family would fluctuate from month to month—blindly spending every cent in the checking account one month, and panicking over the least expense the next. Terri explains, "Now I know what we can afford and what we can't. If there's an unexpected expense, I transfer the money out of other envelopes, and we tighten our belts in those areas until next month."

Terri shares one specific example that demonstrates how to use the envelope budgeting method for periodic expenses, such as the quarterly trash bill. Each quarter this bill seemed to sneak up on the Hamilton family, and Terri would find herself stressed about how to quickly come up with the necessary funds. "Now it's programmed into my envelope system," says Terri. "For the first two months of the quarter, the budgeting system sets aside one-third of the trash bill costs into my "Trash Collection" envelope. When the third month arrives, the remaining amount is allocated and the funds are there and ready for paying the bill. No stress!

"Adopting the envelope budgeting system has done such a good job of freeing me from my financial fog, in fact, that I'm making a major life change. I am starting my own small business. I'm keeping my day job for now, but I'm already getting paid in my side venture! And the envelope budgeting system will help me figure out when I'm making enough in my small business to switch to it full-time." ■

When you commit yourself to using an envelope budgeting system, you become dedicated to living within your means. One of the primary reasons is that the envelope system requires you to set aside money in advance for each of the spending requirements you have, including monthly required and discretionary expenses, as well as periodic required and discretionary expenses. Many people in our society live paycheck to paycheck. The envelope system helps eliminate this problem, because the funding for spending comes from available cash resources that are allocated to envelope spending accounts before the actual spending takes place. After following this system for just a few months, you can quickly get to the point where you have enough money set aside at the beginning of the month to meet all of that month's spending requirements.

Money *for* Life

Applied Principle 9, pages 69–74

One of the significant problems people face today is not understanding how future spending requirements have an impact on their monthly cash flow—certainly the case for Terri Hamilton. For example, have you ever had an annual insurance payment sneak up and surprise you? Other periodic spending requirements include vacations, property tax payments, holiday spending, gifts, auto registration fees, auto maintenance fees, house maintenance expenses, furniture and appliance replacement costs, and so on. When you think about it, many things can catch you off guard if you don't plan ahead.

Most people manage spending through their checking or savings account balance at their bank. Unfortunately, this account balance doesn't prepare you for the periodic spending needs that will inevitably arise in coming months. It also does not alert you to the spending that your partner is planning over the next few days or weeks. So you make independent decisions about how much you think you can spend without really understanding the big picture. This is a very dangerous approach and often leads to problems, including bounced checks, frustration, and ultimately, more debt.

Most overspending in families can be traced to an inability to incorporate periodic spending requirements into their current cash resources and spending practices. A great example of this is the amount of credit card debt that is created during the holidays or on vacations each year as a result of not having money set aside in advance. Many justify this spending by telling themselves they will pay the credit card balance next month. However, this rarely happens because next month's spending requirements are already based on 100 percent of the cash resources for that month.

The envelope system addresses this problem of periodic spending requirements by allowing you to set aside money in advance of periodic spending needs. For example, if you were going to spend $2,400 on Christmas each year, you would be setting aside $200 each month. Stated another way: If you want to spend $2,400 each year for Christmas, you have to spend $200 less on other things each month throughout the year.

Imagine how you will feel each December when you're prepared to purchase gifts for the holidays, and the holiday gift envelope is full! Imagine how you will feel when you want to take a vacation and you know that the money is already set aside in advance. Or imagine how nice it will feel to know that you have money set aside to replace the tires on your car the next time it's required. These are the feelings that Terri Hamilton and her family are now experiencing after using an envelope budgeting system for just a short period of time.

To continue on your financial fitness path during week 7, you will need to track each of your transactions, just as you have been since beginning your envelope budgeting program. Check and date each of the following actions when you have completed them for the week.

■ ACTION 1—WEEK 7: Record All Deposits *(See Action 5, Week 1, page 46.)*

Record all deposits on your bank account registers and appropriately allocate them to each of your envelope spending accounts according to your monthly income allocation plan. Record the appropriate amount on each of your envelope spending account registers.

Check ________ Date ____________________

■ ACTION 2—WEEK 7: Track All Expenses *(See Action 5, Week 1, page 46.)*

Track all expense transactions for the week by recording them on the appropriate bank account register and envelope spending account registers.

Check ________ Date ____________________

■ ACTION 3—WEEK 7: Track All Credit Card Transactions *(See Action 5, Week 1, page 46.)*

Track all credit card transactions for the week by recording them on the appropriate credit card account register, envelope spending account registers, and credit card repayment register.

Check ________ Date ____________________

■ ACTION 4—WEEK 7: Check Your Balances *(See Action 6, Week 1, page 55.)*

Make appropriate spending decisions by spending from the balance remaining in each of your envelope spending accounts. Make any appropriate envelope spending account transfers to other envelope spending accounts.

Check ________ Date ____________________

Way to go—one more week down! Let's move on to week 8.

Track

Success Story

Each month Diane Christianson found herself dreading trying to pay the bills, track her spending, and balance the joint accounts that she shares with Rob, her partner. Diane was using a common software system to download account balances but was writing checks and trying to keep the papers, bills, and account statements all straight in a filing cabinet. Bills would get lost, be paid late, or even be paid twice on occasion. Needless to say, it was quite a feat to figure out where the money went each month.

Along with trying to keep the household running smoothly, Diane also works full-time in the computer industry. In addition to her normal workload, she is working toward a CCNA certification that is critical to her career. The weight of work, studies, and finances were definitely more than she wanted on her shoulders all at once.

When Diane started using the computer-based method of envelope budgeting, many welcome changes started taking place. No longer did paying the bills and balancing the checkbook bring apprehension. Diane states, "I check the envelope system about every other night, and I don't dread it! I can concentrate on my studies instead of where I lost track of all my money."

With the computer-based envelope system, Diane has only one place to go to see her spending, pay the bills, check account balances, and review Rob's spending too. "I can focus on the important task of not overspending instead of constantly going to different Web sites and losing my way." Diane adds, "And since the envelope budgeting system collects all our transactions from our checking accounts and credit cards, I can keep track of Rob's spending too. It really helps us work together to manage our spending."

Online bill paying, along with the transaction tracking and spending plan elements of the envelope system, have truly helped Diane and Rob get control of their finances. When they have overspent in one category, it's clearly highlighted in red. No question about the balance; it's right there, plain to see. No bouncing checks, no missing bills, no late fees.

Now that Diane and Rob are in control, they are well on their way to financial fitness. Using an envelope-based budgeting system has not only lightened their load but has had a positive impact on the rest of their life as well. ■

By now, you too should be experiencing some of the same feelings shared by Diane and the others who have achieved a much higher level of financial fitness by committing themselves to living within their means through the use of an envelope budgeting system. The added confidence and financial peace is definitely worth the effort.

During week 8, you will need to continue tracking each of your transactions. Check and date each of the following actions when you have completed them for the week.

■ ACTION 1—WEEK 8: Record All Deposits *(See Action 5, Week 1, page 46.)*

Record all deposits on your bank account registers and appropriately allocate them to each of your envelope spending accounts according to your monthly income allocation plan. Record the appropriate amount on each of your envelope spending account registers.

Check ________ Date ____________________

■ ACTION 2—WEEK 8: Track All Expenses *(See Action 5, Week 1, page 46.)*

Track all expense transactions for the week by recording them on the appropriate bank account register and envelope spending account registers.

Check ________ Date ____________________

■ ACTION 3—WEEK 8: Track All Credit Card Transactions *(See Action 5, Week 1, page 46.)*

Track all credit card transactions for the week by recording them on the appropriate credit card account register, envelope spending account registers, and credit card repayment register.

Check ________ Date ____________________

■ ACTION 4—WEEK 8: Check Your Balances *(See Action 6, Week 1, page 55.)*

Make appropriate spending decisions by spending from the balance remaining in each of your envelope spending accounts. Make any transfers between envelope spending accounts that are appropriate.

Check _________ Date _____________________

Way to go—one more week down! Let's move on to week 9.

Compare, Adjust, Plan, and Track

You have now reached your second monthly milestone, and, as before, you need to take time to compare your actual results to your plan and make the appropriate adjustments. After having completed this process at the end of the first month, you should be able to move through the exercises quite smoothly.

Check and date each of the following actions when you have completed them for the week.

■ ACTION 1—WEEK 9: Compare and Make Adjustments

Perform a monthly comparison with the envelope system that you have chosen by completing the following steps.

STEP 1: Review the Balance for Each of Your Envelope Spending Accounts *(See Action 1, Week 5, Step 1, page 65.)*

The first step is to review your envelope spending account balances. Determine how much is left in each envelope spending account at the end of the month and how much was spent throughout the month. You need to make sure these calculations include any money transferred from other envelope spending accounts. If you are using the paper ledger system, you will need to complete the Monthly Summary Worksheet. If you are using Mvelopes® Personal, print and review the envelope summary by month report. Compare the amount actually spent during the month with the amount that you had planned to spend. Make any adjustments in your monthly income allocations that are appropriate. Add or delete any envelope spending accounts as necessary.

Check ________ Date ___________________

STEP 2: Transfer Your Savings and Set New Beginning Balances

(See Action 1, Week 5, Step 2, page 69.)

Now that you have completed the review of your envelope spending account balances and made appropriate income allocation adjustments, you need to set the beginning balances for each envelope spending account. Make appropriate envelope spending account transfers to set your beginning balances for next month. Review the criteria for making these transfers and adjustments, as well as setting the beginning balances outlined in *Action 1, Week 5, Step 2, page 69.*

Check ________ Date __________________

STEP 3: Reconcile Your Envelope Spending Accounts and Bank Accounts *(See Action 1, Week 5, Step 3, page 73.)*

Complete a reconciliation of each of your bank accounts. Once completed, make any adjustments that are necessary. Make sure that the total cumulative balance of your bank accounts is equal to the total cumulative balance of your envelope spending accounts.

Check ________ Date __________________

■ ACTION 2—WEEK 9: Complete the Monthly Allocation History Worksheet

(See Action 2, Week 5, page 74.)

You have just completed your second trip around the Success Cycle. You should now be very comfortable with this process. Once you have completed your adjustments for the second month, your plan should be quite accurate. If you are using the paper ledger system, you will need to complete the Monthly Allocation History Worksheet. If you are using Mvelopes Personal, all of the adjustments you have just made have been recorded and your new monthly spending plan has been set.

Check ________ Date __________________

■ ACTION 3—WEEK 9: Prepare the Monthly Income Allocation Plan *(See Action 2, Week 5, page 74.)*

After updating the monthly allocation history, your next step is to prepare a new monthly income allocation plan. If you are using the paper ledger system, complete the Monthly Income Allocation Worksheet. If you are using Mvelopes

Personal, all of the adjustments that you have just made have been recorded and your new monthly income allocation plan has been set.

Check ________ Date ____________________

■ ACTION 4—WEEK 9: Create a Debt Elimination Plan *(See Action 3, Week 5, page 75.)*

Update the Debt Payment Summary Worksheet by recording the payments made for each debt during this past month.

Check ________ Date ____________________

■ ACTION 5—WEEK 9: Record All Deposits

Record all deposits on your bank account registers and appropriately allocate them to each of your envelope spending accounts according to your monthly income allocation plan. Record the appropriate amount on each of your envelope spending account registers.

Check ________ Date ____________________

■ ACTION 6—WEEK 9: Track All Expenses

Track all expense transactions for the week by recording them on the appropriate bank account register and envelope spending account registers.

Check ________ Date ____________________

■ ACTION 7—WEEK 9: Track All Credit Card Transactions

Track all credit card transactions for the week by recording them on the appropriate credit card account register, envelope spending account registers, and credit card repayment register.

Check ________ Date ____________________

■ ACTION 8—WEEK 9: Check Your Balances

Make appropriate spending decisions by spending from the balance remaining in each of your envelope spending accounts. Make any transfers between envelope spending accounts that are appropriate.

Check _________ Date ____________________

We are two-thirds finished with our 12-week program. You can now confidently move on to week 10!

Track

During week 10, you will need to continue tracking each of your transactions. Check and date each of the following actions when you have completed them for the week.

■ ACTION 1—WEEK 10: Record All Deposits *(See Action 5, Week 1, page 46.)*

Record all deposits on your bank account registers and appropriately allocate them to each of your envelope spending accounts according to your monthly income allocation plan. Record the appropriate amount on each of your envelope spending account registers.

Check _________ Date ____________________

■ ACTION 2—WEEK 10: Track All Expenses *(See Action 5, Week 1, page 46.)*

Track all expense transactions for the week by recording them on the appropriate bank account register and envelope spending account registers.

Check _________ Date ____________________

■ ACTION 3—WEEK 10: Track All Credit Card Transactions *(See Action 5, Week 1, page 46.)*

Track all credit card transactions for the week by recording them on the appropriate credit card account register, envelope spending account registers, and credit card repayment register.

Check _________ Date ____________________

■ ACTION 4—WEEK 10: Check Your Balances *(See Action 6, Week 1, page 55.)*

Make appropriate spending decisions by spending from the balance remaining in each of your envelope spending accounts. Make any transfers between envelope spending accounts that are appropriate.

Check ________ Date ____________________

Way to go—only two weeks to go!

Track

During week 11, you will need to continue tracking each of your transactions. Check and date each of the following actions when you have completed them for the week.

■ ACTION 1—WEEK 11: Record All Deposits *(See Action 5, Week 1, page 46.)*

Record all deposits on your bank account registers and appropriately allocate them to each of your envelope spending accounts according to your monthly income allocation plan. Record the appropriate amount on each of your envelope spending account registers.

Check ________ Date ____________________

■ ACTION 2—WEEK 11: Track All Expenses *(See Action 5, Week 1, page 46.)*

Track all expense transactions for the week by recording them on the appropriate bank account register and envelope spending account registers.

Check ________ Date ____________________

■ ACTION 3—WEEK 11: Track All Credit Card Transactions *(See Action 5, Week 1, page 46.)*

Track all credit card transactions for the week by recording them on the appropriate credit card account register, envelope spending account registers, and credit card repayment register.

Check ________ Date ____________________

■ ACTION 4—WEEK 11: Check Your Balances *(See Action 6, Week 1, page 55.)*

Make appropriate spending decisions by spending from the balance remaining in each of your envelope spending accounts. Make any transfers between envelope spending accounts that are appropriate.

Check _________ Date ____________________

Congratulations, you're almost there. Only one week to go!

Track

During week 12, you will need to continue tracking each of your transactions. Check and date each of the following actions when you have completed them for the week.

■ ACTION 1—WEEK 12: Record All Deposits *(See Action 5, Week 1, page 46.)*

Record all deposits on your bank account registers and appropriately allocate them to each of your envelope spending accounts according to your monthly income allocation plan. Record the appropriate amount on each of your envelope spending account registers.

Check ________ Date ____________________

■ ACTION 2—WEEK 12 Track All Expenses *(See Action 5, Week 1, page 46.)*

Track all expense transactions for the week by recording them on the appropriate bank account register and envelope spending account registers.

Check ________ Date ____________________

■ ACTION 3—WEEK 12: Track All Credit Card Transactions *(See Action 5, Week 1, page 46.)*

Track all credit card transactions for the week by recording them on the appropriate credit card account register, envelope spending account registers, and credit card repayment register.

Check ________ Date ____________________

■ ACTION 4—WEEK 12: Check Your Balances *(See Action 6, Week 1, page 55.)*

Make appropriate spending decisions by spending from the balance remaining in each of your envelope spending accounts. Make any transfers between envelope spending accounts that are appropriate.

Check ________ Date ___________________

Way to go! To complete the 12-week program, you need only to finish the compare and adjust process one more time. The next section assists you with these actions.

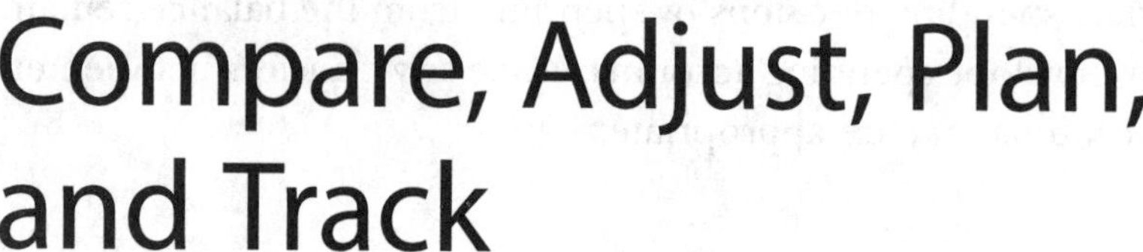

Compare, Adjust, Plan, and Track

You have now reached your third monthly milestone, and, as before, you need to take time to compare your actual results to your plan and make appropriate adjustments.

Check and date each of the following actions when you have completed them for the week.

■ ACTION 1: Compare and Make Adjustments

Perform a monthly comparison with the envelope system that you have chosen by completing the following steps.

STEP 1: Review the Balance for Each of Your Envelope Spending Accounts *(See Action 1, Week 5, Step 1, page 65.)*

The first step is to review your envelope spending account balances. Determine how much is left in each spending account at the end of the month and how much was spent throughout the month. You need to make sure these calculations include any money transferred from other spending accounts. If you are using the paper ledger system, you will need to complete the Monthly Summary Worksheet. If you are using Mvelopes® Personal, print and review the envelope summary by month report. Compare the amount actually spent during the month with the amount that you had planned to spend. Make any adjustments in the your monthly income allocations that are appropriate. Add or delete any spending accounts as necessary.

Check ________ Date ____________________

STEP 2: Transfer Your Savings and Set New Beginning Balances

(See Action 1, Week 5, Step 2, page 69.)

Now that you have completed the review of your spending account balances and made appropriate income allocation adjustments, you need to set the beginning balances for each spending account. Make appropriate envelope to envelope spending account transfers before setting your beginning balances for next month. Review the criteria for making transfers and adjustments in addition to setting the beginning balances outlined in *Action 1, Week 5, Step 2, page 69.*

Check _________ Date ____________________

STEP 3: Reconcile Your Spending Accounts and Bank Accounts

(See Action 1, Week 5, Step 3, page 73.)

Complete a reconciliation of each of your bank accounts. Once completed, make any adjustments that are necessary. Make sure that the total cumulative balance of your bank accounts is equal to the total cumulative balance of your spending accounts.

Check _________ Date ____________________

■ ACTION 2: Compete the Monthly Allocation History *(See Action 2, Week 5, page 74.)*

You have just completed your third trip around the Success Cycle. You should now be very comfortable with this process. Once you have completed your adjustments from the third month, your plan should be quite accurate. If you are using the paper ledger system, you will need to complete the Monthly Allocation History Worksheet. If you are using Mvelopes Personal, all of the adjustments that you have just made have been recorded and your new monthly spending plan has been set.

Check _________ Date ____________________

■ ACTION 3—WEEK 9: Prepare the Monthly Allocation Plan *(See Action 2, Week 5, page 74.)*

After updating the monthly allocation history, your next step is to prepare a new monthly income allocation plan. If you are using the paper ledger system, complete the Monthly Income Allocation Worksheet. If you are using Mvelopes

Personal, all of the adjustments that you have just made have been recorded and your new monthly allocation plan has been set.

Check ________ Date __________________

■ ACTION 4: Update Your Debt Elimination Plan *(See Action 3, Week 5, page 75.)*

Update the Debt Payment Summary Worksheet by recording the payments made for each debt during the past month.

Check ________ Date __________________

■ ACTION 5: Update Your Net-Worth Statement and Review Your Financial Objectives

Update your net-worth statement using one of the blank net-worth statement forms found in Appendix B of the *Success Planner.* Review your progress and make appropriate adjustments to your long-term goals.

Check ________ Date __________________

Congratulations! You have completed your 12-Week *Money for Life* Financial Fitness Program. The steps you have taken have placed you solidly on the path to long-term financial security. If you continue down this path, you will be able to achieve extraordinary results. To prepare yourself well for the future, review the final section of the *Success Planner* and check below when this is completed.

Check ________ Date __________________

Financial Fitness Beyond 12 Weeks

In the book *Money for Life,* Ryan and Christine Richardson were dedicated to completing the 12-week challenge that Tom, a wise financial advisor, had given them. During this time, they were successful in transforming their thinking and in addressing their poor financial habits. Within three short months, the envelope budgeting system created a new way of thinking and allowed them to start living a new way of life.

Obviously, achieving long-term financial fitness is contingent on your ability to consistently apply the principles that you have learned. Successful athletes will tell you that taking off as little as a few weeks from consistent conditioning can be very detrimental to their overall fitness level. Such is the case with financial fitness. If you want to create long-term financial fitness, you must continue applying the principles you have learned. As soon as you stop living within your means, you begin to jeopardize your financial future and the achievement of the goals that you have set. Consistently following the five steps outlined below will help you maintain and enhance your long-term financial fitness:

Money *for* Life
Applied Principle 18, page 133

1. After completing your spending plan adjustments for the third month, continue this process every month. This should always be done together with your partner. Make sure that you continue to live within your means every month. At the end of each month, transfer the amount you have saved in appropriate envelope spending accounts to additional savings, prudent investments, or increased debt reduction.
2. Set aside at least 5 percent of your net monthly income for savings. Consistently increase this amount as you eliminate debt and find other ways to save.
3. After updating your net-worth statement, update it again every 90 days. Review your progress and make appropriate adjustments to your long-term financial goals.
4. After defining your debt elimination plan, update your progress every month and make sure that you are on track with your debt reduction objectives.

5. As you successfully eliminate debt, transfer the amount that you were paying to satisfy debt payments into savings and sound investments. This added amount will assist you greatly in achieving your long-term financial objectives.

THE LIFELONG PURSUIT OF FINANCIAL FITNESS

What does it mean to be physically fit? For some, being physically fit means having the strength and endurance necessary to win a marathon; for others, it means simply the ability to finish. Although some want to be able to compete at a professional level, most agree that being physically fit simply means having a level of fitness necessary to look good, enjoy a healthy life, and be able to participate comfortably in the activities they like. There is no predefined point at which we suddenly become physically fit. Physical fitness is more about being on the right path and doing the right things through proper diet and exercise than it is reaching some magical point in time. However, having specific and attainable objectives that provide motivation for continual improvement is very important. Otherwise, we may struggle with direction and find it difficult to stay on the right path.

Money *for* Life
"The Principles of Money for Life," pages 134–36

Financial fitness is also more about being on the right path than it is about reaching some magical number on a net-worth statement. Clearly, it is more a state of mind than a specific level of wealth. And like the concept of physical fitness, setting appropriate goals and objectives provides the motivation for continual improvement. Most people know if they need to become more financially fit; this is knowledge that generally stems from their daily interaction with issues surrounding money.

In the book *Money for Life,* Ryan and Christine found that most other things in their life were taking a backseat because of the constant stress and strain from poor financial health. However, within a few short weeks of changing directions and following the 12-week *Money for Life* Financial Fitness Program, they found this stress and strain replaced with excitement, relief, and peace. After spending so much time and energy worrying about paying the next bill, running out of money before the end of the month, an ever-increasing debt load, and "maxing out" their credit cards, Ryan and Christine were able to focus attention on the things in life that were most important—including their relationship, their children, and their future.

Perhaps financial fitness can best be measured by how we feel as we interact with money on a daily basis. The following is a list of the many thoughts and feelings that await you as you continue taking the steps necessary to be financially fit for life:

- You have money set aside for the holidays before the shopping begins.
- As you take your next vacation, you know that it is completely paid for before you leave.

- The next time a major appliance needs to be replaced, you have the money already set aside.
- You are able to go to work every day knowing that if you lose your job or have a major illness, you have sufficient emergency funds set aside to carry you through.
- Next year when school starts, you are able to purchase school clothes and supplies from money that is already set aside.
- You never need to worry about checking the account balance at the bank before you pay a bill.
- You are excited to get the next credit card statement, because you know that the balance is shrinking, and if any purchases have been made, you already have the money set aside to pay off those items in full.
- Picking up the mail every day is not a drudgery, because you know that all of the bills coming in are just part of your spending plan and have been anticipated in advance.
- You look forward to making decisions regarding the education of your children, because you are actively saving money for this purpose.
- You spend time planning and anticipating retirement, because you are debt free and prudently investing money to fund the lifestyle you want to have.
- Financial discussions with your partner are more focused on reviewing progress and planning for the future than on the last credit card statement, late bill, or emotionally charged purchase.
- You find it appealing to have financial discussions rather than practicing an avoidance strategy and hoping somehow that the problems will just magically disappear.
- The next time you make a major purchase like an automobile or a house, you are more excited about having completed the purchase within the guidelines of your financial plan than the specific details of what was purchased.
- The last thought on your mind as you drift off to sleep is about how much fun your upcoming vacation will be rather than about how you'll be able to make ends meet.

Being able to have these thoughts and feelings is not contingent on the amount of money you make or your net worth. You do not have to be rich to enjoy this level of financial peace and happiness. Now that you have completed the 12-Week *Money for Life* Financial Fitness Program, you have begun to see the benefits that come from applying these lifelong principles. The only question you have to address now is, Will I continue to take the steps necessary to pursue the path to lifelong financial fitness? The *Money for Life Success Planner* helped you implement important principles that are necessary to achieve the peace and happiness that is reserved for those who make this commitment and complete the 12-week financial fitness program. This program is dedicated to those who have a dream to pursue, the vision to plan, the courage to run, the expectation to perfect, and the persistence to win! Congratulations on your completion of the *Money for Life* Financial Fitness Program. This program is dedicated to you!

Mvelopes® Personal: An Envelope System for Today's World

Mvelopes® Personal is a tool being used by thousands to successfully implement the envelope principles on a daily basis. When Tom met with Ryan and Christine, he introduced them to a computer and Internet-based system that automated the envelope process. This was very important to them because of the complexities associated with managing finances in today's world. As our society becomes less dependent on traditional forms of payment and more focused on cashless spending tools, it is important to utilize a tool that allows you to create a context for decision making by appropriately incorporating all types of spending from all types of accounts.

Attached to the inside back cover of the book *Money for Life,* you will find a CD containing the setup information necessary to use the Mvelopes Personal system. The system has been provided to you to use risk free for 30 days. To begin using Mvelopes Personal, simply insert the CD into the CD-ROM drive of your computer and follow the activation instructions. If you don't have the Mvelopes Personal CD or the CD that you have is not usable, please go to http://www.mvelopes.com/moneyforlife to enroll or to find out more about Mvelopes Personal.

Mvelopes Personal allows you to successfully implement the envelope concepts outlined in this book. As you begin using the system, it assists you with defining your initial spending plan, automatically tracks all of your transactions, automatically updates your envelope spending account balances, and allows you to make timely and appropriate adjustments.

A brief description of the key features and benefits of the Mvelopes Personal system follows.

■ EASILY CREATE A BUDGET: Your Spending Plan

Mvelopes allows you to simply and easily define your monthly income and then set up spending accounts, or envelopes, to which you allocate that income. When you receive a paycheck, Mvelopes lets you split the amount between the various spending accounts you have set up. Spending categories are completely up to you. You can create as many envelopes as you need, and you can group them under category headings as you see fit. For example, the automobile expenses group may contain envelopes for gasoline, repairs, and insurance. By creating envelopes for periodic expenses, such as vacations, car registration fees, or an emergency fund, you can set aside money today for your future spending requirements. Setting a portion of your income aside each month means that the money will be there when periodic expenses are incurred, so you don't have to increase your debt to meet these spending requirements.

■ MANAGE YOUR SPENDING WITH ANYTIME, ANYWHERE ACCESS TO YOUR BUDGET

An advantage to Mvelopes Personal is that it's an online budgeting system, which means you aren't tied to your home computer. You and your partner can have anytime, anywhere access to your budget through the Mvelopes secure online service, so both of you can be looking at your daily spending activity at the same time—at work, at home, on the road, or anywhere you have Internet access. As with Ryan and Christine, when both of you stay involved in the budgeting process, you can count on being successful. Mvelopes allows you to securely and easily access your information from anywhere, providing you with the ability to make informed spending decisions.

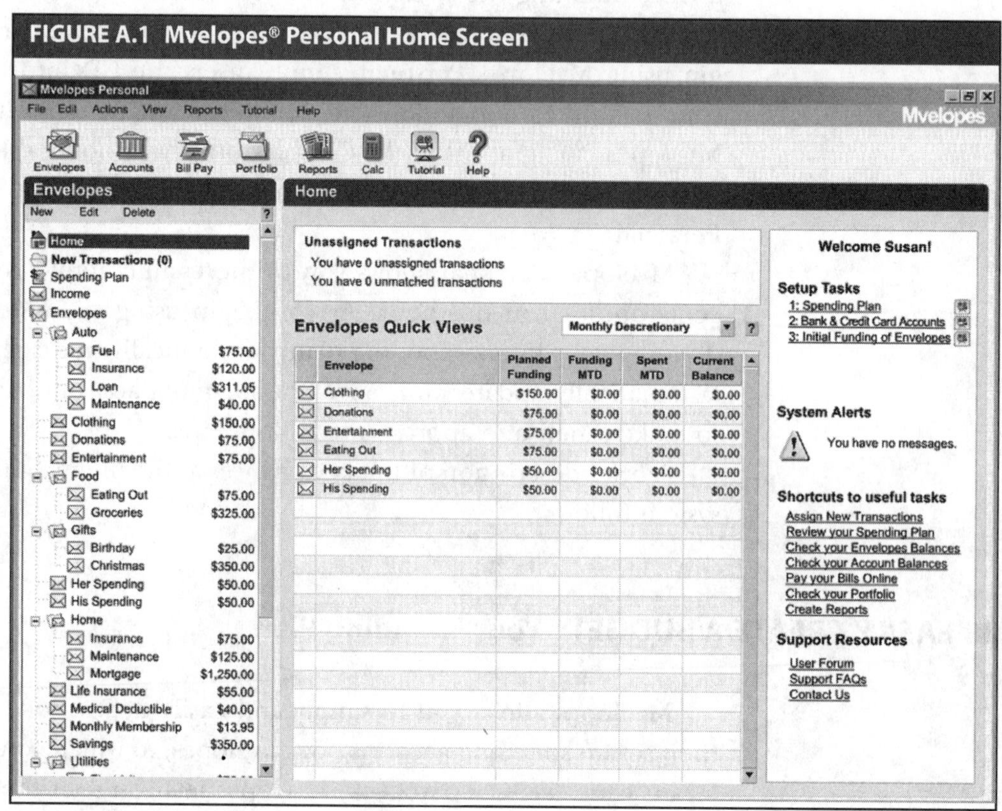

FIGURE A.1 Mvelopes® Personal Home Screen

■ EASILY TRACK ALL YOUR SPENDING

Mvelopes automatically retrieves all of your spending and deposit transactions on a daily basis from your bank, credit union, or credit card company, thus bringing all of your transactions into one place for you to see.

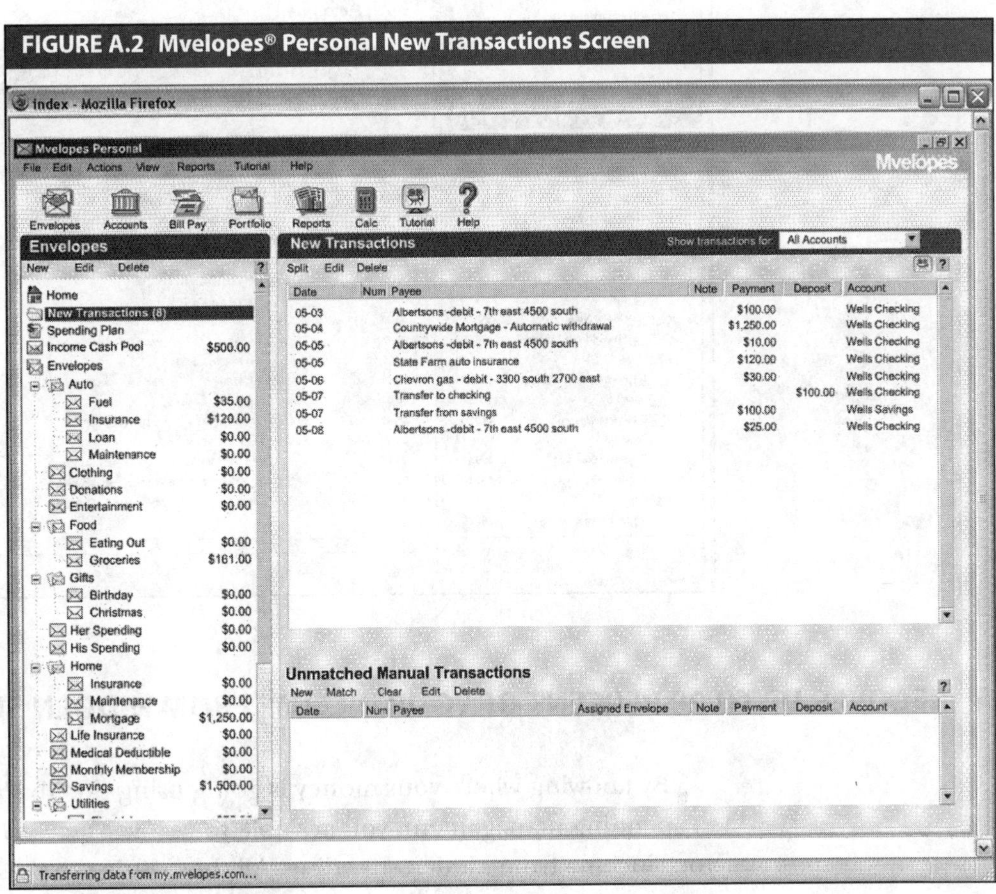

FIGURE A.2 Mvelopes® Personal New Transactions Screen

The interaction you have with each transaction makes managing your spending easy. Mvelopes retrieves each of your transactions from all of your online banking and credit accounts. Each transaction is assigned to an envelope, where the expense is deducted from the income that you allocated to that envelope. You are then able to see your balance and know exactly how much you have left to spend in each envelope spending account. By always knowing exactly how much you have left to spend, you can make better spending decisions.

FIGURE A.3 Mvelopes® Personal Envelope Register Screen

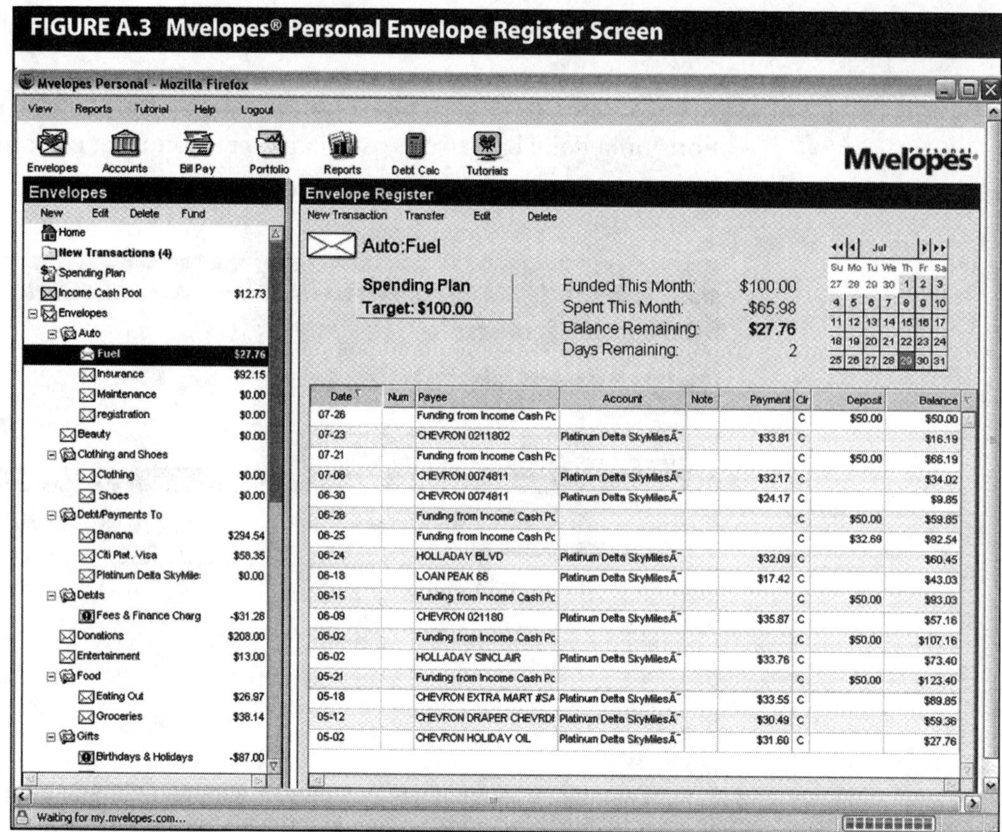

■ RECOVER UP TO 20 PERCENT OF YOUR INCOME FROM HIDDEN SPENDING

By knowing where your money is going using the Mvelopes unique approach to spending management, you are able to recover between 10 and 20 percent of your income from hidden spending. All those little purchases can add up to more than you realize! With better tracking and forecasting, you can recover that money. For example, on the basis of a $40,000 salary over the course of a year, 10 percent would be an extra $4,000 to use for debt reduction, savings, or investments.

■ AUTOMATICALLY PAY ALL OF YOUR BILLS ONLINE

Included in the Mvelopes online budgeting system is a complete online bill payment service—no more writing checks, licking stamps, or going to the post office. Payments can be made manually, can be set up for automatic payment each month, or can be made with the arrival of an electronic bill. The service allows you up to 20 payments a month, which could save you more than $7 a month in postage alone. Payments can be made to any company, store, financial institution, utility company, or individual, eliminating missed payments and late fees.

FIGURE A.4 Mvelopes® Personal Bill Pay Screen

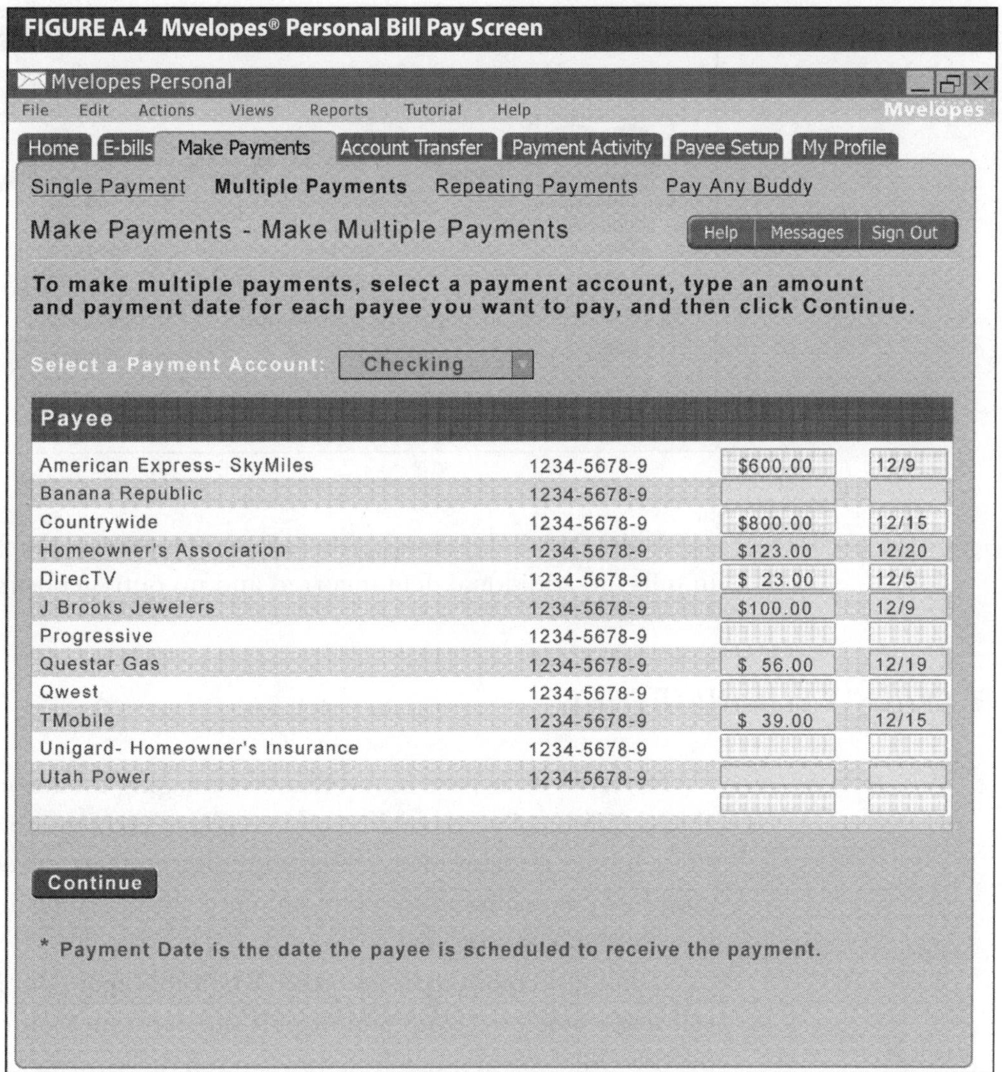

■ EFFECTIVELY MANAGE CREDIT CARD SPENDING WITHOUT ADDING ADDITIONAL DEBT

In today's society, credit cards are often used as an income source instead of as a convenient spending tool. Consequently, there is usually no income available at the end of the month to pay off the debt. Mvelopes manages credit card purchasing by automatically moving allocated funds from your spending envelopes to a credit card repayment envelope every time you use your card. Here's how it works: When you use your credit card to pay for dinner at a local restaurant, that transaction is received into Mvelopes and assigned to your DINING OUT envelope. That amount is then deducted from the DINING OUT envelope and placed into your credit card repayment envelope.

FIGURE A.5 Mvelopes® Personal Credit Card Tracking

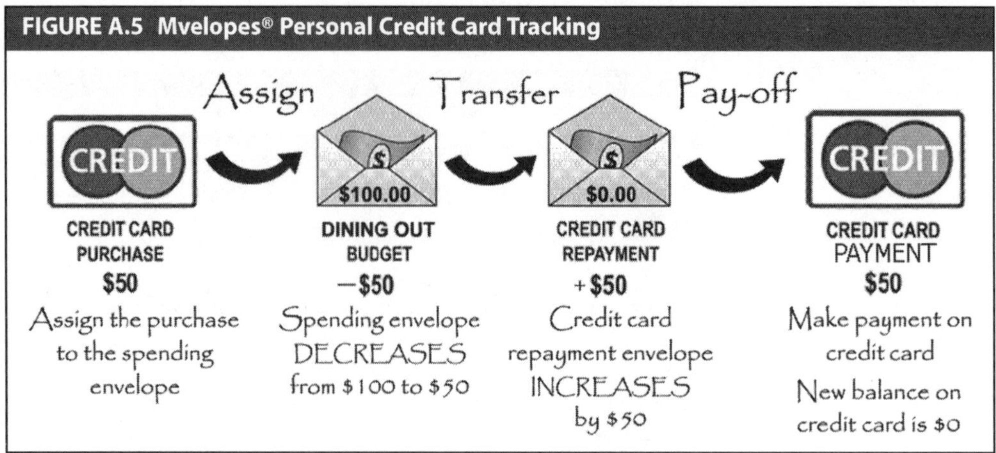
Assign
Transfer
Pay-off
CREDIT
$100.00
$0.00
CREDIT
CREDIT CARD PURCHASE
$50
Assign the purchase to the spending envelope
DINING OUT BUDGET
−$50
Spending envelope DECREASES from $100 to $50
CREDIT CARD REPAYMENT
+$50
Credit card repayment envelope INCREASES by $50
CREDIT CARD PAYMENT
$50
Make payment on credit card
New balance on credit card is $0

At the end of the month, you have money set aside to pay off your credit card in full—no additional debt incurred and no outrageous interest payments.

QUICKLY ELIMINATE DEBT

Mvelopes users have found that by managing their spending closely, they are able to eliminate overspending and even save extra money each month. In many cases, money remains in several of your discretionary envelopes at the end of the month. By sweeping those extra amounts into current debt payments, you can quickly eliminate your debt.

If you have more than one debt, when that first debt is paid in full, you can roll that whole payment amount plus the extra into your next priority debt on the list. Once you are debt free, you can roll those former debt payments into savings and investments to provide a more financially stable future for yourself and your family.

MANAGE YOUR COMPLETE PORTFOLIO

Track all of your investments from Mportfolio™, so that you can see the big picture from one summary page. As an integral part of your Mvelopes Personal budgeting system, you can customize Mportfolio to access and track all of your investment accounts, such as IRAs, 401(k)s, and mutual funds. This summary page allows you to see your complete financial picture in one quick snapshot, rather than surfing around to several different sites to see the balances in all your varying accounts. Should you want to make changes to an account, you can simply click on that account to access the screen where you can make the appropriate adjustments.

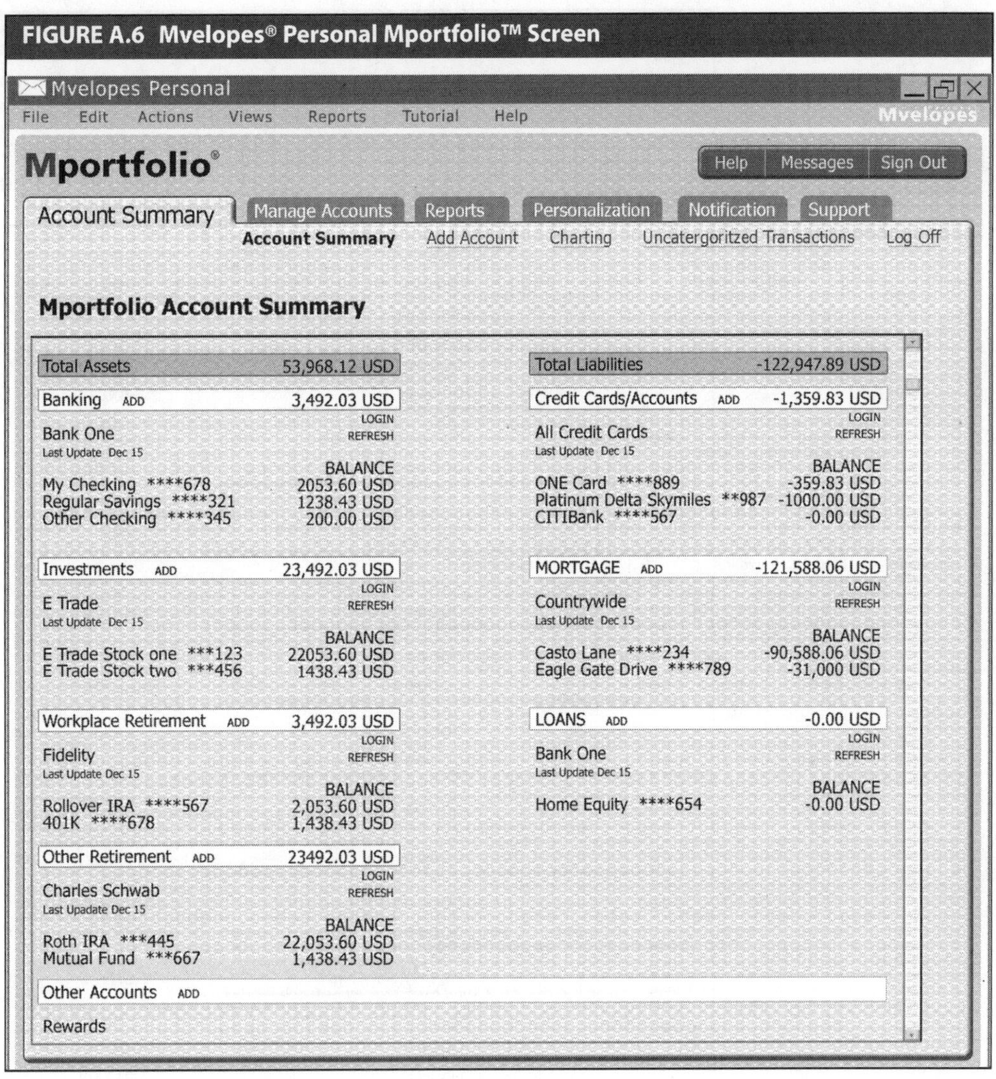

FIGURE A.6 Mvelopes® Personal Mportfolio™ Screen

■ GENERATE CLEAR, INFORMATIVE REPORTS

With Mvelopes Personal, you can generate any number of reports that will help you see where you are in your quest to become financially fit. These reports make everything easier, from doing your taxes to planning a special event or even to just reviewing your financial status. Reports can be generated in numerous ways:

- Search for transactions by payee or by date.
- Review transactions or envelope registers for a certain day, week, or month.
- Calculate what portion of your expenses are in a particular category.
- Compare income allocation against actual expenses for any envelope category by day, month, and year.
- View the current status of your envelopes and accounts with the monthly allocation, balance, and current spending.

FIGURE A.7 Mvelopes® Personal Summary Report

Mvelopes Summary Report

Group Name	Mvelope Name	Monthly allocation	Spent this month	Current balance
	Childcare	$180.00	$0.00	$180.00
	Clothing	$150.00	$56.25	$93.75
	Donations	$30.00	$0.00	$30.00
	Household	$100.00	$0.00	$100.00
	Miscellaneous	$50.00	$0.00	$50.00
	Savings	$408.17	$0.00	$408.17
Allowances	Me	$50.00	$0.00	$50.00
	Spouse	$50.00	$0.00	$50.00
Auto	Gas & Oil	$133.00	$25.00	$108.00
	Registration	$33.33	$0.00	$166.69
Debt/Payments To	American Express	$0.00	$23.87	$123.87
	Citibank VISA	$60.00	$0.00	$60.00
Debts	Car Payments	$630.00	$0.00	$630.00
	Mortgage	$1,200.00	$0.00	$1,200.00
Entertainment	Cable & Internet	$50.00	$0.00	$50.00
	Movies/Events	$125.00	$8.10	$116.90
Financial Plan	College Fund	$50.00	$0.00	$50.00
	IRA	$100.00	$0.00	$100.00
	Investments	$100.00	$0.00	$100.00
Food	Dining Out	$140.00	$23.87	$116.13
	Groceries	$415.00	$0.00	$415.00
Health	Co-Pay/Supplies	$75.00	$0.00	$75.00
Insurance	Auto	$100.00	$0.00	$500.00
	Health	$100.00	$0.00	$100.00
	Housing	$41.00	$0.00	$41.00
	Life	$110.00	$0.00	$110.00
System	Monthly Funding	$0.00	$0.00	$979.14
	Shortfall	$0.00	$0.00	$0.00
Taxes	Property Taxes	$100.00	$0.00	$100.00
Utilities	Electricity	$111.00	$0.00	$111.00
	Gas	$36.00	$0.00	$36.00
	Mobile Phone	$50.00	$0.00	$50.00
	Phone	$72.00	$0.00	$72.00
	Water	$38.00	$0.00	$38.00
	Totals	**$4,887.50**	**$137.09**	**$6,410.65**

■ RECEIVE UNLIMITED CUSTOMER SUPPORT AND BUDGET COACHING

Included with your Mvelopes online service is unlimited telephone support and coaching, as well as access to our message boards, FAQs, tutorials, and e-mail support. Users also receive a monthly online newsletter with tips for using the Mvelopes system and other useful financial fitness suggestions.

■ AUTOMATIC FEATURE UPGRADES AT NO ADDITIONAL COST

Any upgrades to the Mvelopes online budgeting system are included free of charge to all Mvelopes members—no more worrying about paying for and upgrading to the next version of software.

■ SUMMARY

For additional information, please visit http://www.mvelopes.com. If you are looking for a financial advisor, educator, or coach who understands the Mvelopes Personal system and would like contact information, please go to http://www.mvelopes.com/resources and simply find the resource most suited to your needs.

Forms

Appendix B contains all the forms that you will need to execute your 12-Week *Money for Life* Financial Fitness Plan. You may want to use these forms as a master copy and make photocopies to use as necessary, while you continue down the path toward financial fitness.

FIGURE B.1

Financial Fitness Quiz Scorecard

1 ____________________

2 ____________________

3 ____________________

4 ____________________

5 ____________________

6 ____________________

7 ____________________

8 ____________________

9 ____________________

10 ____________________

11 ____________________

12 ____________________

13 ____________________

14 ____________________

15 ____________________

16 ____________________

17 ____________________

18 ____________________

19 ____________________

20 ____________________

21 ____________________

22 ____________________

23 ____________________

24 ____________________

25 ____________________

A = 1 Points	_____ A × 1 = _____
B = 3 Points	_____ B × 3 = _____
C = 5 Points	_____ C × 5 = _____
	Total: _____

Score	Level of Financial Fitness
30 or Less	Very High
31 to 50	High
51 to 70	Moderate
71 to 100	Low
101 to 125	Very Low

Financial Fitness Quiz Scorecard

1 ____________________

2 ____________________

3 ____________________

4 ____________________

5 ____________________

6 ____________________

7 ____________________

8 ____________________

9 ____________________

10 ____________________

11 ____________________

12 ____________________

13 ____________________

14 ____________________

15 ____________________

16 ____________________

17 ____________________

18 ____________________

19 ____________________

20 ____________________

21 ____________________

22 ____________________

23 ____________________

24 ____________________

25 ____________________

A = 1 Points	_____ A × 1 = _____
B = 3 Points	_____ B × 3 = _____
C = 5 Points	_____ C × 5 = _____
	Total: _____

Score	Level of Financial Fitness
30 or Less	Very High
31 to 50	High
51 to 70	Moderate
71 to 100	Low
101 to 125	Very Low

FIGURE B.1

Financial Fitness Quiz Scorecard	Financial Fitness Quiz Scorecard
1 ______	1 ______
2 ______	2 ______
3 ______	3 ______
4 ______	4 ______
5 ______	5 ______
6 ______	6 ______
7 ______	7 ______
8 ______	8 ______
9 ______	9 ______
10 ______	10 ______
11 ______	11 ______
12 ______	12 ______
13 ______	13 ______
14 ______	14 ______
15 ______	15 ______
16 ______	16 ______
17 ______	17 ______
18 ______	18 ______
19 ______	19 ______
20 ______	20 ______
21 ______	21 ______
22 ______	22 ______
23 ______	23 ______
24 ______	24 ______
25 ______	25 ______
A = 1 Points ______ A × 1 = ______	A = 1 Points ______ A × 1 = ______
B = 3 Points ______ B × 3 = ______	B = 3 Points ______ B × 3 = ______
C = 5 Points ______ C × 5 = ______	C = 5 Points ______ C × 5 = ______
Total: ______	**Total**: ______

Score	Level of Financial Fitness
30 or Less	Very High
31 to 50	High
51 to 70	Moderate
71 to 100	Low
101 to 125	Very Low

Score	Level of Financial Fitness
30 or Less	Very High
31 to 50	High
51 to 70	Moderate
71 to 100	Low
101 to 125	Very Low

FIGURE B.2

Personal Net-Worth Statement		
Assets	**Value of Asset**	
Cash-Equivalent		
Total Cash-Equivalent		
Real Estate		
Total Real Estate		
Other		
Total Other		
Total Assets (Cash-Equivalent + Real Estate + Other)		
Liabilities	**Amount of Liability**	
Total Liabilities		
Net Worth (Total Assets – Total Liabilities)		

FIGURE B.2

Personal Net-Worth Statement				
Assets	Value of Asset			
Cash-Equivalent				
Total Cash-Equivalent				
Real Estate				
Total Real Estate				
Other				
Total Other				
Total Assets (Cash-Equivalent + Real Estate + Other)				
Liabilities	Amount of Liability			
Total Liabilities				
Net Worth (Total Assets – Total Liabilities)				

FIGURE B.3

Variable Net Income						
Income Source						
Payment Number	Income 1		Income 2		Income 3	
Total						
Average Check Amount						
Lowest Check Amount						
To calculate the Average Check Amount, divide the Total by the number of checks received.						

Variable Net Income						
Income Source						
Payment Number	Income 1		Income 2		Income 3	
Total						
Average Check Amount						
Lowest Check Amount						
To calculate the Average Check Amount, divide the Total by the number of checks received.						

FIGURE B.3

Variable Net Income						
Income Source						
Payment Number	Income 1		Income 2		Income 3	
Total						
Average Check Amount						
Lowest Check Amount						
To calculate the Average Check Amount, divide the Total by the number of checks received.						

Variable Net Income						
Income Source						
Payment Number	Income 1		Income 2		Income 3	
Total						
Average Check Amount						
Lowest Check Amount						
To calculate the Average Check Amount, divide the Total by the number of checks received.						

FIGURE B.4

Monthly Net Income — Date: ____________

Fixed Net Income				
Income Source	Net Amount of Income	Pay Periods per Year	Annual Net Income	Monthly Net Income
Total Fixed Net Income				

Variable Net Income				
Income Source	Average Net Amount of Check	Pay Periods per Year	Annual Net Income	Monthly Net Income
Total Variable Net Income				
Total Monthly Net Income (Fixed Net Income + Variable Net Income)				

Monthly Net Income — Date: ____________

Fixed Net Income				
Income Source	Net Amount of Income	Pay Periods per Year	Annual Net Income	Monthly Net Income
Total Fixed Net Income				

Variable Net Income				
Income Source	Average Net Amount of Check	Pay Periods per Year	Annual Net Income	Monthly Net Income
Total Variable Net Income				
Total Monthly Net Income (Fixed Net Income + Variable Net Income)				

FIGURE B.4

Monthly Net Income				Date: ____________
Fixed Net Income				
Income Source	Net Amount of Income	Pay Periods per Year	Annual Net Income	Monthly Net Income
Total Fixed Net Income				
Variable Net Income				
Income Source	Average Net Amount of Check	Pay Periods per Year	Annual Net Income	Monthly Net Income
Total Variable Net Income				
Total Monthly Net Income (Fixed Net Income + Variable Net Income)				

Monthly Net Income				Date: ____________
Fixed Net Income				
Income Source	Net Amount of Income	Pay Periods per Year	Annual Net Income	Monthly Net Income
Total Fixed Net Income				
Variable Net Income				
Income Source	Average Net Amount of Check	Pay Periods per Year	Annual Net Income	Monthly Net Income
Total Variable Net Income				
Total Monthly Net Income (Fixed Net Income + Variable Net Income)				

FIGURE B.5

Monthly Spending Plan — Month: ________________

Monthly Envelope Spending Accounts

Monthly Required Accounts	Annual Spending		Monthly Allocation		Monthly Discretionary Accounts	Annual Spending		Monthly Allocation	
Total—Monthly Required					Total—Monthly Discretionary				

Periodic Envelope Spending Accounts

Periodic Required Accounts	Annual Spending		Monthly Allocation		Periodic Disrectionary Accounts	Annual Spending		Monthly Allocation	
Total—Periodic Required					Total—Periodic Discretionary				

Spending Plan Summary

	Annual		Monthly	
Total Net Monthly Income				
Envelope Spending Accounts				
Total Monthly Required Spending				
Total Monthly Discretionary Spending				
Total Periodic Required Spending				
Total Periodic Discretionary Spending				
Total Monthly Allocation				
Balance (Net Monthly Income – Monthly Allocation)				

FIGURE B.5

Monthly Spending Plan

Month: ________________

Monthly Envelope Spending Accounts					
Monthly Required Accounts	Annual Spending	Monthly Allocation	Monthly Discretionary Accounts	Annual Spending	Monthly Allocation
Total—Monthly Required			Total—Monthly Discretionary		

Periodic Envelope Spending Accounts					
Periodic Required Accounts	Annual Spending	Monthly Allocation	Periodic Disrectionary Accounts	Annual Spending	Monthly Allocation
Total—Periodic Required			Total—Periodic Discretionary		

Spending Plan Summary		
Total Net Monthly Income	Annual	Monthly
Envelope Spending Accounts		
Total Monthly Required Spending		
Total Monthly Discretionary Spending		
Total Periodic Required Spending		
Total Periodic Discretionary Spending		
Total Monthly Allocation		
Balance (Net Monthly Income – Monthly Allocation)		

FIGURE B.6

Bank Account Register | Bank Account: ____________________

Date	Transaction ID Number	Transaction Description	Deposit +		Expense –		Cleared	Balance	

FIGURE B.6

Bank Account Register

Bank Account: ______________________

Date	Transaction ID Number	Transaction Description	Deposit +	Expense –	Cleared	Balance

FIGURE B.7

Envelope Spending Account Register

Envelope Spending Account: ______________________

Date	Transaction ID Number	Transaction Description	Deposit +		Expense –		Balance	

FIGURE B.7

Envelope Spending Account Register

Envelope Spending Account: ______________________

Date	Transaction ID Number	Transaction Description	Deposit +		Expense –		Balance	

FIGURE B.8

Cash Account Register Cash Account: ____________________

Date	Transaction Description	Deposit +		Expense –		Balance	

FIGURE B.8

Cash Account Register Cash Account: ____________________

Date	Transaction Description	Deposit +		Expense –		Balance	

FIGURE B.9

Credit Card Account Register

Credit Card Account: ______________________________

Date	Transaction ID Number	Transaction Description	Deposit +	Expense –	Cleared	Balance

FIGURE B.9

Credit Card Account Register

Credit Card Account: ________________________

Date	Transaction ID Number	Transaction Description	Deposit +		Expense –		Cleared	Balance	

FIGURE B.10

Credit Card Repayment Register

Credit Card Account: ______________________

Date	Transaction ID Number	Transaction Description	Deposit +	Expense –	Balance

FIGURE B.10

Credit Card Repayment Register — Credit Card Account: ____________________

Date	Transaction ID Number	Transaction Description	Deposit +		Expense –		Balance	

FIGURE B.11

Initial Allocation—Beginning Balance for Envelope Spending Accounts

Date: ________

Monthly Envelope Spending Accounts

Monthly Required Accounts	Beginning Balance		Monthly Discretionary Accounts	Beginning Balance	

Periodic Envelope Spending Accounts

Periodic Required Accounts	Beginning Balance		Periodic Discretionary Accounts	Beginning Balance	

Total Balance of Accounts (Bank Account and Actual Cash on Hand)		
Total Allocated to Envelope Spending Accounts		
Balance (Total Balance of Accounts – Total Allocated to Envelope Spending Accounts)		

FIGURE B.11

Initial Allocation—Beginning Balance for Envelope Spending Accounts Date: _________

Monthly Envelope Spending Accounts			
Monthly Required Accounts	Beginning Balance	Monthly Discretionary Accounts	Beginning Balance
Periodic Envelope Spending Accounts			
Periodic Required Accounts	Beginning Balance	Periodic Discretionary Accounts	Beginning Balance
Total Balance of Accounts (Bank Account and Actual Cash on Hand)			
Total Allocated to Envelope Spending Accounts			
Balance (Total Balance of Accounts – Total Allocated to Envelope Spending Accounts)			

FIGURE B.12

Monthly Income Allocation Plan

Date: ____________________

Income Source							
Date of Receipt							
Amount of Income							
Envelope Spending Accounts	Monthly Spending Plan	Allocation Amount	Allocation Amount	Allocation Amount	Allocation Amount	Allocation Amount	Allocation Amount
Monthly Required							
Monthly Discretionary							
Periodic Required							
Periodic Discretionary							
Total Allocations:							

FIGURE B.12

Monthly Income Allocation Plan Date: ____________________

	Income Source						
	Date of Receipt						
	Amount of Income						
Envelope Spending Accounts	Monthly Spending Plan	Allocation Amount	Allocation Amount	Allocation Amount	Allocation Amount	Allocation Amount	Allocation Amount
Monthly Required							
Monthly Discretionary							
Periodic Required							
Periodic Discretionary							
Total Allocations:							

FIGURE B.12

Monthly Income Allocation Plan — Date: ____________________

Income Source							
Date of Receipt							
Amount of Income							
Envelope Spending Accounts	Monthly Spending Plan	Allocation Amount	Allocation Amount	Allocation Amount	Allocation Amount	Allocation Amount	Allocation Amount
Monthly Required							
Monthly Discretionary							
Periodic Required							
Periodic Discretionary							
Total Allocations:							

FIGURE B.12

Monthly Income Allocation Plan — Date: ____________________

	Income Source						
	Date of Receipt						
	Amount of Income						
Envelope Spending Accounts	Monthly Spending Plan	Allocation Amount	Allocation Amount	Allocation Amount	Allocation Amount	Allocation Amount	Allocation Amount
Monthly Required							
Monthly Discretionary							
Periodic Required							
Periodic Discretionary							
Total Allocations:							

FIGURE B.12

Monthly Income Allocation Plan — Date: ______________________

Income Source							
Date of Receipt							
Amount of Income							
Envelope Spending Accounts	Monthly Spending Plan	Allocation Amount	Allocation Amount	Allocation Amount	Allocation Amount	Allocation Amount	Allocation Amount
Monthly Required							
Monthly Discretionary							
Periodic Required							
Periodic Discretionary							
Total Allocations:							

FIGURE B.12

Monthly Income Allocation Plan Date: ______________________

Income Source							
Date of Receipt							
Amount of Income							
Envelope Spending Accounts	Monthly Spending Plan	Allocation Amount	Allocation Amount	Allocation Amount	Allocation Amount	Allocation Amount	Allocation Amount
Monthly Required							
Monthly Discretionary							
Periodic Required							
Periodic Discretionary							
Total Allocations:							

FIGURE B.12

Monthly Income Allocation Plan Date: ____________

	Income Source						
	Date of Receipt						
	Amount of Income						
Envelope Spending Accounts	Monthly Spending Plan	Allocation Amount	Allocation Amount	Allocation Amount	Allocation Amount	Allocation Amount	Allocation Amount
Monthly Required							
Monthly Discretionary							
Periodic Required							
Periodic Discretionary							
Total Allocations:							

FIGURE B.12

Monthly Income Allocation Plan Date: ______________________

Income Source							
Date of Receipt							
Amount of Income							
Envelope Spending Accounts	**Monthly Spending Plan**	**Allocation Amount**	**Allocation Amount**	**Allocation Amount**	**Allocation Amount**	**Allocation Amount**	**Allocation Amount**
Monthly Required							
Monthly Discretionary							
Periodic Required							
Periodic Discretionary							
Total Allocations:							

FIGURE B.12

Monthly Income Allocation Plan — Date: ______________

Income Source							
Date of Receipt							
Amount of Income							
Envelope Spending Accounts	Monthly Spending Plan	Allocation Amount	Allocation Amount	Allocation Amount	Allocation Amount	Allocation Amount	Allocation Amount
Monthly Required							
Monthly Discretionary							
Periodic Required							
Periodic Discretionary							
Total Allocations:							

FIGURE B.12

Monthly Income Allocation Plan Date: ______________________

Envelope Spending Accounts	Monthly Spending Plan	Allocation Amount	Allocation Amount	Allocation Amount	Allocation Amount	Allocation Amount	Allocation Amount
Income Source							
Date of Receipt							
Amount of Income							
Monthly Required							
Monthly Discretionary							
Periodic Required							
Periodic Discretionary							
Total Allocations:							

FIGURE B.13

Monthly Envelope Spending Account Summary — Date: ______________

Envelope Spending Accounts	Monthly Spending Plan	Amount Spent	Remaining Balance	Spending Plan Adjustments	New Monthly Spending Plan
Monthly Required					
Monthly Discretionary					
Periodic Required					
Periodic Discretionary					
Total:					

FIGURE B.13

Monthly Envelope Spending Account Summary

Date: ____________________

Envelope Spending Accounts	Monthly Spending Plan		Amount Spent		Remaining Balance		Spending Plan Adjustments		New Monthly Spending Plan	
Monthly Required										
Monthly Discretionary										
Periodic Required										
Periodic Discretionary										
Total:										

FIGURE B.13

Monthly Envelope Spending Account Summary

Date: ____________________

Envelope Spending Accounts	Monthly Spending Plan	Amount Spent	Remaining Balance	Spending Plan Adjustments	New Monthly Spending Plan
Monthly Required					
Monthly Discretionary					
Periodic Required					
Periodic Discretionary					
Total:					

FIGURE B.13

Monthly Envelope Spending Account Summary — Date: ____________

Envelope Spending Accounts	Monthly Spending Plan	Amount Spent	Remaining Balance	Spending Plan Adjustments	New Monthly Spending Plan
Monthly Required					
Monthly Discretionary					
Periodic Required					
Periodic Discretionary					
Total:					

FIGURE B.13

Monthly Envelope Spending Account Summary — Date: ____________________

Envelope Spending Accounts	Monthly Spending Plan		Amount Spent		Remaining Balance		Spending Plan Adjustments		New Monthly Spending Plan	
Monthly Required										
Monthly Discretionary										
Periodic Required										
Periodic Discretionary										
Total:										

FIGURE B.13

Monthly Envelope Spending Account Summary

Date: ____________________

Envelope Spending Accounts	Monthly Spending Plan	Amount Spent	Remaining Balance	Spending Plan Adjustments	New Monthly Spending Plan
Monthly Required					
Monthly Discretionary					
Periodic Required					
Periodic Discretionary					
Total:					

FIGURE B.13

Monthly Envelope Spending Account Summary Date: ____________

Envelope Spending Accounts	Monthly Spending Plan	Amount Spent	Remaining Balance	Spending Plan Adjustments	New Monthly Spending Plan
Monthly Required					
Monthly Discretionary					
Periodic Required					
Periodic Discretionary					
Total:					

FIGURE B.13

Monthly Envelope Spending Account Summary

Date: ____________________

Envelope Spending Accounts	Monthly Spending Plan		Amount Spent		Remaining Balance		Spending Plan Adjustments		New Monthly Spending Plan	
Monthly Required										
Monthly Discretionary										
Periodic Required										
Periodic Discretionary										
Total:										

FIGURE B.13

Monthly Envelope Spending Account Summary Date: ____________________

Envelope Spending Accounts	Monthly Spending Plan	Amount Spent	Remaining Balance	Spending Plan Adjustments	New Monthly Spending Plan
Monthly Required					
Monthly Discretionary					
Periodic Required					
Periodic Discretionary					
Total:					

FIGURE B.13

Monthly Envelope Spending Account Summary

Date: ____________________

Envelope Spending Accounts	Monthly Spending Plan	Amount Spent	Remaining Balance	Spending Plan Adjustments	New Monthly Spending Plan
Monthly Required					
Monthly Discretionary					
Periodic Required					
Periodic Discretionary					
Total:					

FIGURE B.14

Monthly Allocation History

Month: ____________________

Funding from Income	
Funding from Savings	
Total Funding	

Envelope Spending Accounts	Monthly Allocation Amount from Spending Plan	Amount Underfunded from Previous Month	Total Funding Required	Monthly Funding	Amount Underfunded
Monthly Required					
Monthly Discretionary					
Periodic Required					
Periodic Discretionary					
Total:					

Income Holding Account (For Use with Variable Income Flows)

Beginning Balance	
Deposits	
Withdrawals	
Ending Balance	

FIGURE B.14

Monthly Allocation History Month: ____________

Funding from Income	
Funding from Savings	
Total Funding	

Envelope Spending Accounts	Monthly Allocation Amount from Spending Plan	Amount Underfunded from Previous Month	Total Funding Required	Monthly Funding	Amount Underfunded
Monthly Required					
Monthly Discretionary					
Periodic Required					
Periodic Discretionary					
Total:					

Income Holding Account (For Use with Variable Income Flows)

Beginning Balance	
Deposits	
Withdrawals	
Ending Balance	

FIGURE B.14

Monthly Allocation History Month: ____________

Funding from Income	
Funding from Savings	
Total Funding	

Envelope Spending Accounts	Monthly Allocation Amount from Spending Plan	Amount Underfunded from Previous Month	Total Funding Required	Monthly Funding	Amount Underfunded
Monthly Required					
Monthly Discretionary					
Periodic Required					
Periodic Discretionary					
Total:					

Income Holding Account (For Use with Variable Income Flows)

Beginning Balance	
Deposits	
Withdrawals	
Ending Balance	

FIGURE B.14

Monthly Allocation History — Month: ____________

Funding from Income	
Funding from Savings	
Total Funding	

Envelope Spending Accounts	Monthly Allocation Amount from Spending Plan	Amount Underfunded from Previous Month	Total Funding Required	Monthly Funding	Amount Underfunded
Monthly Required					
Monthly Discretionary					
Periodic Required					
Periodic Discretionary					
Total:					

Income Holding Account (For Use with Variable Income Flows)

Beginning Balance	
Deposits	
Withdrawals	
Ending Balance	

FIGURE B.14

Monthly Allocation History Month: ____________

Funding from Income	
Funding from Savings	
Total Funding	

Envelope Spending Accounts	Monthly Allocation Amount from Spending Plan	Amount Underfunded from Previous Month	Total Funding Required	Monthly Funding	Amount Underfunded
Monthly Required					
Monthly Discretionary					
Periodic Required					
Periodic Discretionary					
Total:					

Income Holding Account (For Use with Variable Income Flows)

Beginning Balance	
Deposits	
Withdrawals	
Ending Balance	

FIGURE B.14

Monthly Allocation History Month: ______________

Funding from Income	
Funding from Savings	
Total Funding	

Envelope Spending Accounts	Monthly Allocation Amount from Spending Plan	Amount Underfunded from Previous Month	Total Funding Required	Monthly Funding	Amount Underfunded
Monthly Required					
Monthly Discretionary					
Periodic Required					
Periodic Discretionary					
Total:					

Income Holding Account (For Use with Variable Income Flows)

Beginning Balance	
Deposits	
Withdrawals	
Ending Balance	

FIGURE B.14

Monthly Allocation History

Month: ____________

Funding from Income	
Funding from Savings	
Total Funding	

Envelope Spending Accounts	Monthly Allocation Amount from Spending Plan	Amount Underfunded from Previous Month	Total Funding Required	Monthly Funding	Amount Underfunded
Monthly Required					
Monthly Discretionary					
Periodic Required					
Periodic Discretionary					
Total:					

Income Holding Account (For Use with Variable Income Flows)

Beginning Balance	
Deposits	
Withdrawals	
Ending Balance	

FIGURE B.14

Monthly Allocation History Month: ______________________

Funding from Income	
Funding from Savings	
Total Funding	

Envelope Spending Accounts	Monthly Allocation Amount from Spending Plan	Amount Underfunded from Previous Month	Total Funding Required	Monthly Funding	Amount Underfunded
Monthly Required					
Monthly Discretionary					
Periodic Required					
Periodic Discretionary					
Total:					

Income Holding Account (For Use with Variable Income Flows)

Beginning Balance	
Deposits	
Withdrawals	
Ending Balance	

FIGURE B.14

Monthly Allocation History	Month: ______________

Funding from Income	
Funding from Savings	
Total Funding	

Envelope Spending Accounts	Monthly Allocation Amount from Spending Plan	Amount Underfunded from Previous Month	Total Funding Required	Monthly Funding	Amount Underfunded
Monthly Required					
Monthly Discretionary					
Periodic Required					
Periodic Discretionary					
Total:					

Income Holding Account (For Use with Variable Income Flows)

Beginning Balance	
Deposits	
Withdrawals	
Ending Balance	

FIGURE B.14

Monthly Allocation History

Month: ______________________

Funding from Income	
Funding from Savings	
Total Funding	

Envelope Spending Accounts	Monthly Allocation Amount from Spending Plan	Amount Underfunded from Previous Month	Total Funding Required	Monthly Funding	Amount Underfunded
Monthly Required					
Monthly Discretionary					
Periodic Required					
Periodic Discretionary					
Total:					

Income Holding Account (For Use with Variable Income Flows)

Beginning Balance	
Deposits	
Withdrawals	
Ending Balance	

FIGURE B.15

Debt Summary — Date: ____________

Debt Description	Balance		Payment		Interest Rate

FIGURE B.15

Debt Summary					Date: ____________
Debt Description	Balance		Payment		Interest Rate

FIGURE B.16

Debt Payment Summary

Debt Priority Order	Debt:		Debt:		Debt:		Debt:		Debt:		Debt:	
Description of Debt												
Month												
Month												
Month												
Month												
Month												
Month												
Month												
Month												
Month												
Month												
Month												
Month												
Month												
Month												
Month												
Month												
Month												
Month												
Month												
Month												
Month												
Month												
Month												
Month												
Month												
Month												
Month												
Month												
Month												
Month												
Month												
Month												
Month												

FIGURE B.16

Debt Payment Summary

Debt Priority Order	Debt:		Debt:		Debt:		Debt:		Debt:		Debt:	
Description of Debt												
Month												
Month												
Month												
Month												
Month												
Month												
Month												
Month												
Month												
Month												
Month												
Month												
Month												
Month												
Month												
Month												
Month												
Month												
Month												
Month												
Month												
Month												
Month												
Month												
Month												
Month												
Month												
Month												
Month												
Month												
Month												
Month												
Month